French Grammar For Beginners

Learn French Grammar Through English Comparisons

French Hacking

Copyright © 2024 French Hacking

All rights reserved. No part of this publication may be reproduced, distributed or transmitted in any form or by any means, including photocopying, recording, or other electronic or mechanical methods, without the prior written permission of the publisher, except in the case of brief quotations embodied in critical reviews and certain other non-commercial uses permitted by copyright law.

Trademarked names appear throughout this book. Rather than use a trademark symbol with every occurrence of a trademarked name, names are used in an editorial fashion, with no intention of infringement of the respective owner's trademark. The information in this book is distributed on an "as is" basis, without warranty. Although every precaution has been taken in the preparation of this work, neither the author nor the publisher shall have any liability to any person or entity with respect to any loss or damage caused or alleged to be caused directly or indirectly by the information contained in this book.

"One language sets you in a corridor for life. Two languages open every door along the way."

- Frank Smith

French Hacking

French Hacking is a revolutionary educational language learning company focused on teaching individuals how to learn French in the shortest time possible. Our mission is for our students to develop a command of the French language by utilizing the hacks, tips, and tricks included in the learning materials we create. We want our students to become confident in their speaking abilities as they advance their conversational skills by teaching what's necessary without having to learn the finer details that don't make much of a difference or aren't even used in the real world.

Unlike our competitors, who have books geared toward multiple languages, our language learning books are dedicated exclusively to learning French. Our focus on only one language allows us to truly concentrate on creating superior educational materials.

Our books are created by native French speakers and then put through a vigorous editing process with two more native French editors and proofreaders to ensure the highest quality content. Rest assured that you are learning proper grammar and syntax as you read through our books.

The unique formatting of our books will give you the best experience possible as you learn French! The bilingual English and French text appear side-by-side for easy reference without needing a dictionary. With fun images for each chapter, you will better visualize the scenes within the story and stay engaged. Reading is an immersive experience, and we want to make learning fun and enjoyable.

There are no other books like ours on the market. Let us help accelerate your journey to learn French with our fun and effective educational materials that make learning French a breeze!

About this book

This book offers a distinctive approach to mastering French grammar by providing clear explanations and practical examples, all through the lens of English grammar. This comprehensive, easy-to-follow guide presents each grammar concept in English with its counterpart explanations in French, accompanied by examples illustrating both languages. Our goal is to provide you with an authentic and straightforward way to learn French grammar, making it easier to understand through direct comparisons to English.

Who's it for?

This book is designed for students who are just starting out learning French and want a general, digestible knowledge of French grammar.

BONUS!

Enhance your learning experience by downloading the free audiobook and PDF version of this book. As an extra bonus, you also get our online French course with over 250 video lessons and downloadable PDFs! For more details, please refer to the last page.

Enjoy learning and exploring these valuable resources at your convenience!

Table of Contents

Chapter 1: What Is in a Word? 1
Chapter 2: Nouns 4
Chapter 3: Gender 6
Chapter 4: Number 10
Chapter 5: Articles 13
Chapter 6: The Possessive 19
Chapter 7: Verbs 21
Chapter 8: The Infinitive 23
Chapter 9: Subjects 26
Chapter 10: Pronouns 28
Chapter 11: Subject Pronouns 30
Chapter 12: Verb Conjugation 36
Chapter 13: Auxiliary Verbs 46
Chapter 14: Affirmative and Negative Sentences 49
Chapter 15: Declarative and Interrogative Sentences 53
Chapter 16: Tenses 57
Chapter 17: The Present Tense 60
Chapter 18: Participles 62
Chapter 19: The Past Tense 66
Chapter 20: The Past Perfect Tense 73
Chapter 21: The Future Tense 76
Chapter 22: The Future Perfect Tense 80
Chapter 23: Moods 83
Chapter 24: The Imperative 85
Chapter 25: The Conditional 88
Chapter 26: The Subjunctive 94
Chapter 27: Adjectives 101
Chapter 28: Descriptive Adjectives 103
Chapter 29: Comparison of Adjectives 107

Chapter 30: Possessive Adjectives 111
Chapter 31: Interrogative Adjectives 117
Chapter 32: Demonstrative Adjectives 119
Chapter 33: Adverbs 121
Chapter 34: Conjunctions 124
Chapter 35: Prepositions 127
Chapter 36: Objects 130
Chapter 37: Direct Object Pronouns 137
Chapter 38: Indirect Object Pronouns 141
Chapter 39: Disjunctive Pronouns 147
Chapter 40: Reflexive Pronouns and Verbs 154
Chapter 41: Possessive Pronouns 159
Chapter 42: Interrogative Pronouns 165
Chapter 43: Relative Pronouns 174
Chapter 44: Demonstrative Pronouns 188
Chapter 45: Active and Passive Voice 194

CHAPTER 1: WHAT IS IN A WORD?

> **ILLUSTRATIVE EXAMPLE**
>
> English: *The* **curious cat swiftly jumped over the tall fence because** *it* **saw a bird.** *It* **balanced itself,** *then* **pounced.** *The* **agile feline landed gracefully, catching** *the* **bird off guard.**
>
> French: Le **chat curieux** a **sauté rapidement par-dessus** la **haute clôture parce qu'il** a **vu** un **oiseau.** Il **s'est équilibré,** puis a **bondi.** L'**agile félin** a **atterri gracieusement, attrapant l'oiseau par surprise.**

When you learn a foreign language, in this case French, you must look at each word in four ways: *meaning, part of speech, function,* and *form.*

Meaning

An English word may be connected to a French word that has a similar meaning. *Boy*, a young male child, has the same meaning as the French word *garçon*. Words with equivalent meanings are learned by memorizing vocabulary.

Every language has expressions where the meaning of a group of words is different from the meaning of words taken individually. These are called **Idiomatic Expressions** or **Idioms**. For example, in English, *to fall asleep* and *to take a walk* don't mean the same as *to fall down the stairs* or *to take a book to school*. You need to watch out for idioms because you can't translate them word-for-word into French.

>*to rain cats and dogs* → **pleuvoir des cordes**
>(word-for-word *"to rain ropes"*)
>
>*to hit the nail on the head* → **taper dans le mille**
>(word-for-word *"to hit in the thousand"*)

Part of Speech

In English and in French, words are grouped according to how they are used in a sentence. There are eight groups corresponding to eight **Parts of Speech**:

1. Nouns
2. Articles
3. Verbs
4. Adverbs

5. Pronouns
6. Prepositions
7. Adjectives
8. Conjunctions

Some parts of speech are divided into different types. For example, adjectives can be descriptive, interrogative, demonstrative, or possessive. Each part of speech has its own rules for spelling, pronunciation, and usage.

To choose the right French word for an English word, you need to know its part of speech. For example, look at the word "plays" in these two sentences. In each sentence, *plays* is a different part of speech, so it translates to a different word in French.

>Mary *plays* chess.
>>Verb → **joue**

>Mary reads *plays*.
>>Noun → **pièces**

This handbook will help you identify parts of speech so you can choose the correct French words and know the rules for using them.

Function

In English and in French the role a word plays in a sentence is called **Function**. For example, words that are nouns can have the following functions:

- Subject
- Direct object
- Indirect object
- Object of a preposition

To choose the right French word for an English word, you need to know its function. For example, look at the word *him* in these two sentences. In each sentence, it has a different function, so it translates to a different French word.

>Jack watches *him*.
>>Whom does Alex watch? **Him** → direct object → **le**

>Jack gives *him* the pen.
>>To whom Alex gives the pen? *Him* → indirect object → **lui**

This handbook will help you understand the function of words so you can choose the correct French words and know the rules for using them.

Form

In English and French, a word can change the form of another word, like its spelling and pronunciation. This is called **Agreement**, meaning one word matches or "agrees" with another.

>I am → *am* agrees with *I*
>She is → *is* agrees with *she*

Agreement does not play a big role in English, but it is an important part of the French language. As an example, look at the sentences below where the bold indicates which words must agree with one another.

>*This blue* **handbag belongs** *to my aunt.*
>Ce **sac à main** bleu **appartient** à ma tante.

In English, the only word that affects another word in the sentence is *handbag*, which forces us to say *belongs*. If we change *handbag* to *handbags*, we would have to say *belong* to make it agree with *handbags*.

In French, the word for *handbag* (**sac à main**) not only impacts both the spelling and pronunciation of *belongs* (**appartient**), but also of the words *the* (**le**) and *blue* (**bleu**). The word for *aunt* (**tante**) affects the spelling and pronunciation of the French word for *my* (**ma**).

As we introduce different parts of speech in this handbook, we will explain **Agreement**. You'll learn which words need to agree with each other and how to show this agreement.

FRENCH FACT: SILENT LETTERS

In French, many words have silent letters, especially at the end. For example, **beaucoup** (meaning *a lot*) is pronounced as *"boh-coo"* and **chat** (*cat*) is pronounced as *"sha."*

Chapter 2: Nouns

> **ILLUSTRATIVE EXAMPLE**
>
> <u>English</u>: *The **dog** chased the **cat** through the **garden** and into the **house**, where it found a cozy **bed**.*
>
> <u>French</u>: Le **chien** a poursuivi le **chat** à travers le **jardin** et dans la **maison**, où il a trouvé un **lit** confortable.

A **Noun** is a word that can be the name of a person, animal, place, thing, event, or idea.

- **A person:** professor, clown, student, girl, Julia, Alex, Daniel, Jade.
- **An animal:** dog, bird, bear, snake, Spot, Tweetie, Teddy.
- **A place:** city, state, country, continent, stadium, restaurant, France, Europe.
- **A thing:** lamp, airplane, iPad, dress, Perrier, Eiffel Tower, Arch of Triumph.
- **An event or activity:** graduation, marriage, birth, death, football, robbery, rest, growth.
- **An idea or concept:** poverty, democracy, humor, mathematics, addition, strength, elegance, virtue.

As you can see, a noun is not just a word for something you can touch, like a lamp, dog, or book. It can also name things you can't touch, like poverty, mathematics, and virtue.

A **Common Noun** is a general name for a person, place, thing, etc. It does not start with a capital letter unless it's the first word of a sentence. All the lowercase words above are common nouns.

A **Proper Noun** is the specific name of a person, place, thing, etc. It always starts with a capital letter. All the capitalized words above are proper nouns.

> *Marc* is an *artist*.
> Marc: proper noun
> artist: common noun

A noun made up of two words is called a **Compound Noun**. A compound noun can be two nouns put together, like *coffee table* and *fire station*.

In English
To help you learn to recognize nouns, look at the paragraph below where the nouns

are in italics.

> Some of *people's* favorite French *products* include *wines, soaps, jewelry, perfumes* and other luxury *goods*. But thanks to the *European Union*, you don't actually have to be in *France* to find French *products*. You can find French *cheeses* and *brands* in *Italy* and *Germany*, just like you can find Italian *cars* in *France*.

In French
Nouns are identified in the same way as they are in English.

Terms used to talk about nouns:
- **Gender:** A noun has a gender, meaning it can be classified as masculine, feminine, or neuter (see *Gender*).
- **Number:** A noun has a number, meaning it can be either singular or plural (see *Number*).
- **Count or non-count:** A noun can be a **count noun** or a **non-count noun**. This means it either refers to something that can be counted or something that cannot be counted. (see *Articles*).
- **Function:** A noun can have a variety of functions in a sentence; that is, it can be the **subject** of the sentence (see *Subjects*) or an **object** (see *Objects*).

FRENCH FACT: GENDER OF NOUNS

All French nouns have a gender, either masculine or feminine. For example, **le soleil** (*the sun*) is masculine, but **la lune** (*the moon*) is feminine. This impacts the spelling of adjectives, possessive and demonstrative pronouns, and even participles.

CHAPTER 3: GENDER

> **ILLUSTRATIVE EXAMPLE**
>
> English: *The beautiful pink flower lies magnificently in the sunny garden, while the summer sun gently warms the fresh air of the morning.*
>
> French: **La** belle **fleur** rose se trouve magnifiquement dans **le jardin** ensoleillé, tandis que **le soleil** d'été réchauffe doucement **l'air** frais du matin.

In grammar, **Gender** means a word can be classified as *masculine, feminine,* or *neuter*.

> Did Angela give Marc the wallet?
> Yes, *she* gave *it* to him.
>   she: feminine
>   it: neuter
>   him: masculine

Gender is not very important in English, but it is at the heart of the French language. In French, the gender of a word affects how it is spelled and pronounced, as well as how related words are spelled and pronounced.

Each part of speech in French has its own rules for indicating gender. You will learn about gender in the chapters on articles, pronouns, and adjectives. In this section, we will only look at the gender of nouns.

In English
Nouns don't have a gender themselves, but sometimes their meaning suggests a gender based on the biological sex of the person or animal they represent. For example, when we replace a noun referring to a man, we use *he*, and for a woman, we use *she*.

- Nouns referring to males indicate the **masculine** gender:
  - *Marc* went on a trip; *he* was thrilled and I was happy for *him*.
    - Marc: noun (male)
    - he: masculine
    - him: masculine

- Nouns referring to females indicate the **feminine** gender:
  - *Vanessa* went to the doctor's; *she* wasn't feeling well and I went with *her*.
    - Vanessa: noun (female)

- she: feminine
- her: feminine

Proper or **common nouns** don't have a biological gender and are considered **neuter**. They are replaced by *it*.

Florence is a beautiful historical *city*, I enjoyed exploring *it*.
Florence: noun
city: noun
it: neuter

In French

All nouns, whether they are common nouns or proper nouns, have a gender; they are either masculine or feminine. But don't mix up the grammatical terms *masculine* and *feminine* with *male* and *female*. While a few French nouns directly relate to the biological sex of a person, most nouns have a gender you need to memorize.

The gender of common and proper nouns tied to biological sex is easy to figure out. These nouns can only refer to one of the biological sexes, male or female.

- **Males: masculine**
    Alex
    boy
    brother
    son

- **Females: feminine**
    Julia
    girl
    sister
    daughter

For both common nouns and proper nouns, you can't guess their gender. They have a **Grammatical Gender** that doesn't relate to biological sex and that needs to be memorized. Here are some examples of English nouns and their gender in French.

- **Masculine**
    office → le bureau
    truck → le camion
    United Kingdom → le Royaume-Uni
    document → le document

- **Feminine**
    television → la télévision

life → la vie
Malaysia → la Malaisie
photo → la photo

When you learn a new noun, remember its gender because it affects how related words are spelled and pronounced. Textbooks and dictionaries usually show a noun's gender with *m.* for masculine or *f.* for feminine. Sometimes, indefinite articles like **un** for masculine or **une** for feminine are used to indicate gender (see *Articles*).

Here is a list of some noun endings that often, but not always, indicate a noun's gender:

Masculine
- **-age** : avantage, garage, bagage (*luggage*)
- **-eau** : gâteau (*cake*), manteau (*coat*), bateau (*boat*)
- **-et** : objet (*object*), secret (*secret*), carnet (*notebook*)
- **-isme** : capitalisme (*capitalism*), tourisme (*tourism*), réalisme (*realism*)
- **-ment** : gouvernement, monument, événement (*event*)
- **-oir** : soir (*evening*), rasoir (*razor*), tiroir (*drawer*)

Feminine
- **-ace** : glace (*ice cream*), place, surface
- **-asse** : impasse (*cul-de-sac*), classe
- **-aison** : maison (*house*), saison (*season*), raison (*reason*)
- **-ance** : tolérance, assurance (*insurance*), substance
- **-ence** : présence, absence, compétence
- **-ade** : promenade (*walk*), escapade, ambassade (*embassy*)
- **-esse** : promesse (*promise*), adresse, richesse (*wealth*)
- **-ette** : cassette, bicyclette, serviette (*napkin*)
- **-ière** : lumière (*light*), bière (*beer*), manière (*manner*)
- **-sion** : télévision, décision, compréhension
- **-tion** : nation, production, compétition
- **-té** : société, liberté, beauté (*beauty*)
- **-tude** : étude (*study*), attitude, solitude
- **-ure** : ceinture (*belt*), nature, peinture (*painting*)

Careful – Don't try to determine a noun's gender based on its ending because there are many exceptions. Always check the gender in your dictionary. Also, don't assume a noun's gender based on the person it refers to. For example, the noun **personne** (*person*) is always feminine in French, even if it refers to a man.

FRENCH FACT: GENDER IN FRENCH PROFESSIONS

French nouns that refer to professions often have both masculine and feminine forms. However, historically, the feminine form was created by adding an **-e, -se** or **-trice** to the masculine form, leading to words like **acteur** (*actor, masculine*) and **actrice** (*actress, feminine*), **acheteur** (*buyer, masculine*) and **acheteuse** (*buyer, feminine*). While this reflects traditional gender roles, efforts are being made to use the masculine form for both genders to promote gender neutrality.

Chapter 4: Number

> **ILLUSTRATIVE EXAMPLE**
>
> English: *The **dog** barks, the **dogs** play. A **cat** sleeps, **cats** meow in the street.*
>
> French: Le **chien** aboie, les **chiens** jouent. Un **chat** dort, des **chats** miaulent dans la rue.

In grammar, **Number** means a word can be classified as singular or plural. If a word refers to one person or thing, it is singular. If it refers to more than one, it is plural.

>one *pen* → singular
>two *pens* → plural

In French, more parts of speech show number (singular or plural) than in English, and French words change their spelling and pronunciation more to indicate this.

Type of words affected by Number:

- **English**
  Nouns
  Verbs
  Pronouns
  Demonstrative adjectives

- **French**
  Nouns
  Verbs
  Pronouns
  Adjectives
  Articles

Each part of speech has its own rules for showing number (singular or plural). You will learn about this in the chapters on articles, adjectives, pronouns, and verbs. In this section, we will only look at the number of nouns.

In English
A singular noun becomes plural in one of two ways:

1. Some singular nouns add an *-s* or *-es*
   book → books

kiss → kisses

2. Other singular nouns change their spelling:
    woman → women
    foot → feet
    tooth → teeth
    goose → geese

Some nouns, called **Collective Nouns**, refer to a group of people or things, but are singular.

This *flock* counts twenty-five birds.
The *herd* of cows is happy.

In French

Just like in English, the plural form of a noun in French is usually spelled differently than the singular form.

The most common change is adding an *-s* to the end of the singular noun, for both masculine and feminine nouns.

	SINGULAR	PLURAL	ENGLISH	
MASCULINE	camion	camions	*truck*	*trucks*
FEMININE	voiture	voitures	*car*	*cars*

As in English, French **Collective Nouns** are considered singular.

Ce **troupeau** compte vingt-cinq oiseaux.
This flock counts twenty-five birds. → flock: singular

Le **troupeau** de vaches est heureux.
The herd of cows is happy. → herd: singular

Some nouns form the plural differently. For example: singular nouns ending in **-al** → **-aux**

animal → animaux (*animal* → *animals*)

Hearing the Plural

In English, you can usually hear the plural in the noun itself.

SINGULAR	PLURAL
the thing	the things
the leaf	the leaves

In French, even though you can see the s at the end of plural nouns, you often don't hear it because it's not pronounced.

Same pronunciation:

SINGULAR	PLURAL
chose	choses
feuille	feuilles

In this situation, you can tell if a noun is singular or plural by listening to the words that come before it, like **le** and **la** for singular or **les** for plural (see *Articles*).

SINGULAR	PLURAL
la chose	les choses
la feuille	les feuilles

FRENCH FACT: PLURALS

In French, most nouns form their plural by adding an **s** to the singular form. For example, **chat** (*cat*) becomes **chats** (*cats*), with the **s** usually not pronounced. There are exceptions to this rule, such as nouns ending in **-eau**, **-eu**, and **-au**, which typically add an **x** instead of **s** to form the plural, like **château** (*castle*) becoming **châteaux** (*castles*).

CHAPTER 5: ARTICLES

> **ILLUSTRATIVE EXAMPLE**
>
> English: *Beneath **the** warm sun, **the** woman buys some bread while **the** boy enjoys a juicy apple. In **the** garden, birds sing among **the** flowers.*
>
> French: Sous **le** chaud soleil, **la** femme achète **du** pain tandis que **le** garçon savoure **une** pomme juteuse. Dans **le** jardin, **les** oiseaux chantent parmi **les** fleurs.

An **Article** is a word placed before a noun indicating whether the noun refers to a specific person, animal, place, thing, event, or idea, or whether it refers to a non specific person, thing, or idea.

> I saw *the* film you told me about.
> the → a specific film
>
> I saw *a* cat in the park.
> a → not a specific cat

In English and in French there are two types of articles: **Definite Articles** and **Indefinite Articles**.

Definite Articles

In English
A **definite article** is used before a noun to refer to a specific person, place, animal, thing, or idea. There is one definite article, ***the***.

> Pass me *the* pen on your desk.
> the → a specific pen
>
> I ate *the* cake you bought earlier.
> the → a specific cake

The definite article remains *the* even when the noun that follows is plural.

> Pass me *the pens* on your desk.
> I ate *the cakes* you bought earlier.

In French

As in English, a definite article is placed before a French noun to refer to a specific person, place, animal, thing, or idea.

> Passe-moi **le** stylo sur ton bureau.
> *Pass me **the** pen on your desk.*
>
> J'ai mangé **le** gâteau que tu as acheté tout à l'heure.
> *I ate **the** cake you bought earlier.*

However, in French, there is more than one definite article. The definite article matches the noun's gender and number. This is called **agreement**. We say *the article agrees with the noun* (see *Gender and Number*).

A different article is used depending on whether the noun is *masculine* or *feminine* (gender) and on whether the noun is *singular* or *plural* (number).

There are four forms of the definite article: three singular forms and one plural form.

- *le* indicates that the noun is masculine singular:

le cahier	*the notebook*
le bonbon	*the candy*

- *la* indicates that the noun is feminine singular:

la rose	*the rose*
la glace	*the ice cream*

- **l'** is used instead of **le** and **la** before a word beginning with a **vowel** (sounds associated with the letters a, e, i, (y), o, and u; consonants are the sounds associated with the other letters of the alphabet.). Using **l'** does not indicate if the noun is masculine or feminine:

l'oiseau (masc.)	*the bird*
l'angoisse (fem.)	*the anxiety*

In French, the letter **h** is never pronounced. So, a word starting with **h** is treated like it starts with a vowel and uses **l'** as the definite article: **l'heure** (*the hour*), **l'hôpital** (*the hospital*).

- *les* is used to indicate that the noun is plural. Since there is only one form, it does not indicate if the noun is masculine or feminine.

les desserts	*the desserts*
les fleurs	*the flowers*

You will often have to rely on the different forms of articles to indicate the gender and number of the noun.

Careful – French nouns often need a definite article even when there isn't one in English. Here are some examples.

- When the noun is used to speak in general terms:
  I love wine. → J'adore **le** vin.
  Cats are ferocious. → **Les** chats sont féroces.

- When the noun refers to a concept:
  That's life. → C'est **la** vie.
  Goodness is worth more than beauty. → **La** bonté vaut mieux que **la** beauté.

- The names of countries and geographical areas:
  Belgium → **La** Belgique
  Morocco → **Le** Maroc
  Indonesia → **L'**Indonésie
  China → **La** Chine

Indefinite Articles

In English
An **Indefinite Article** is a word placed before a noun when we are not referring to a specific person, animal, place, thing, event, or idea. There are two indefinite articles: *a* and *an*.

- *a* is used before a word beginning with a **consonant**:

    I saw *a* fox in the garden → not a specific fox

- *an* is used before a word beginning with a **vowel**:

    I had *an* orange for breakfast → not a specific orange

The indefinite article is only used with singular nouns. For non-specific plural nouns, you can use *some* or *any*, but they tend to be left out.

> I ate cupcakes. → I ate (*some*) cupcakes.
> Do you have pets? → Do you have (*any*) pets?

In French

Like in English, an indefinite article is used before a French noun when talking about a non-specific person, place, animal, thing, or idea. Indefinite articles must match the noun's gender and number. There are three forms of the indefinite article: two for singular nouns and one for plural nouns.

- **un** indicates that the noun is masculine singular:

un fruit	*a fruit*
un verre	*a glass*

- **une** indicates that the noun is feminine singular:

une assiette	*a plate*
une carotte	*a carrot*

- **des** is used to show that a noun is plural. It doesn't show if the noun is masculine or feminine because there is only one form. Unlike in English, where *some* can be left out, the French word **des** must be used.

des plats	*some dishes*
des fleurs	*some flowers*

> J'ai mangé **des** plats délicieux.
> *I ate **some** delicious dishes.*

The three forms above, **un**, **une**, and **des**, usually change to **de** when the verb is negated (see *Affirmative and Negative Sentences*).

> J'ai **un** chat → Je n'ai pas **de** chat
> *I have **a** cat → I don't have **a** cat*
>
> J'ai pris **un** dessert → Je n'ai pas pris **de** dessert
> *I had dessert → I didn't have **any** dessert*

J'ai **des** boutons → Je n'ai pas **de** bouton
*I have (**some**) pimples → I don't have **any** pimples*

Careful – Assume that most French nouns are preceded by an article. It is an exception when they aren't.

Non-Count Nouns and Partitive Articles

In English
Common nouns can be divided into two groups: **Count Nouns** and **Non-Count Nouns**.

Count Nouns: As the name implies, count nouns designate objects that can be counted. For example: you can count the noun *apples: one apple, two apples,...* Count nouns can be singular or plural. (On the preceding pages all the examples used for indefinite articles are count nouns.)

Non-Count Nouns: As the name implies, non-count nouns designate objects that cannot be counted; for example, you cannot count the noun *money: one money, two moneys,...* Non-count nouns are always singular.

In English, we don't usually need to distinguish count and non-count nouns because they both use the same articles. But in French, it's important to identify non-count nouns.

In French
Non-count nouns don't use words like indefinite articles. Instead, they use a special set of words called **Partitive Articles**. These articles only have one form for each gender because non-count nouns are always singular. In French, you must use partitive articles, unlike in English where they can be left out.

- **du** is used before a masculine non-count noun:
  J'apporte **du** bois. → *I'm bringing (**some**) wood.*
  Avez-vous **du** jus ? → *Do you have **any** juice?*

- **de la** is used before a feminine noun-count noun:
  J'écoute **de la** musique. → *I am listening to (**some**) music.*
  Avez-vous **de la** musique ? → *Do you have (**any**) music?*

- **de l'** replaces **du** and **de la** before a non-count noun beginning with a vowel.

It does not indicate if the noun is masculine or feminine.

J'ai acheté **de l'**or. → *I bought **(some)** gold.*
Avez-vous **de l'**électricité ? → *Do you have **any** power?*

STUDY TIPS: NOUNS AND THEIR GENDER

Flashcards
- Create a flashcard for each new noun. Write the singular form, and if the plural is irregular, on the French side.
- Use blue for masculine nouns and red for feminine nouns. This will help you remember their gender.
- As you study the flashcards, add an adjective like **intéressant** when saying the French word and article. The pronunciation of the adjective changes depending on if it's with a masculine or feminine noun. This change will help you remember the noun's gender better.

    le musée (intéressant) → *the (interesting) museum*
    la fleur (intéressante) → *the (interesting) flower*
    l'événement (masc.) (intéressant) → *the (interesting) event*
- Don't forget that it is only through repeated use that you will remember the words and their gender.

Chapter 6: The Possessive

> **ILLUSTRATIVE EXAMPLE**
>
> English: In **mom's** flourishing garden, vibrant flowers bloom, while **John's** gleaming car catches the sunlight. Each night, the **cat's** soothing purring lulls us to sleep.
>
> French: Dans le jardin florissant **de maman**, les fleurs éclatantes fleurissent, tandis que la voiture brillante **de John** attrape le soleil. Chaque nuit, le ronronnement apaisant **du chat** nous berce pour dormir.

The term **Possessive** means that one noun owns or possesses another noun.

    Marc's phone is in the kitchen.
        Marc → possessor
        phone → possessed

    The *bird's* wing is broken.
        bird → possessor
        wing → possessed

In English
There are some possessive constructions:

1. With an ***apostrophe***. In this structure, the possessor is placed before the possessed.

- **Singular possessor + apostrophe + s:**
  Jacob's car
  a *bird's* wings

- **Plural possessor ending with s + apostrophe after the s:**
  the *birds'* nests
  the *boys'* group

- **A plural possessor not ending with s + apostrophe + s:**
  the *feet's* smell
  the *women's* clothing

2. With the word ***of***. In this structure, the possessed is placed before the possessor.

- A singular or plural possessor is proceeded by **of the** or **of a**:
  the phone *of the* teacher (singular possessor)

the wings *of a* bird (singular possessor)
the coats *of the* gentlemen (plural possessor)

In French

There is only one possessive construction which is the ***of*** structure (point 2 above). The apostrophe structure (point 1 above) does not exist.

The French structure follows the English structure: the noun possessed + **de** (*of*) + definite or indefinite article + the common noun possessor. If the possessor is a proper noun, there is no preceding article.

> **le costume de John** → *John's suit / the suit of John*
> John → possessor, proper noun
> suit → possessed
>
> **l'ordinateur du patron** → *the boss's computer / the computer of the boss*
> boss → possessor, common noun
> computer → possessed
>
> **le pull de la femme** → *the woman's sweater / the sweater of the woman*
>
> **les nageoires d'un requin** → *a shark's fins / the fins of a shark*
>
> **le patron des employés** → *the employees' boss / the boss of the employees*

Careful – Don't confuse **du, de la, de l'**, and **des** used for possession with the same words used as indefinite and partitive articles meaning *some* or *any*. When these words come between two nouns, they usually indicate possession: *the computer of the boss* → *l'ordinateur du patron*. Otherwise, they are articles: *she eats fruits* → *elle mange des fruits*.

In English and in French, possession can also be indicated using **Possessive Adjectives**, such as **my** house, **his** car → **ma** maison, **sa** voiture (see *Possessive Adjectives*).

FRENCH FACT: INFLUENCE ON ENGLISH
About 30% of English words come from French, due to the Norman Conquest of England in 1066. Words like ballet, café, and entrepreneur are direct imports.

CHAPTER 7: VERBS

> **ILLUSTRATIVE EXAMPLE**
>
> English: The birds **sing** joyfully and the sun **rises**, while the children **laugh** and **play** in the park, **filling** the air with happiness.
>
> French: Les oiseaux **chantent** joyeusement et le soleil **se lève** tandis que les enfants **rient** et **jouent** dans le parc, **remplissant** l'air de bonheur.

A **Verb** is a word that indicates the action of the sentence. The word *action* is used in a broad sense; it doesn't necessarily refer to physical actions.

Let's look at different types of words that are verbs:
- **A physical activity:** to run, to hike, to listen, to jump
- **A mental activity:** to think, to reflect, to brainstorm, to remember
- **A condition:** to be, to feel, to have, to seem

However, many verbs do not fit neatly into one of the three categories above. They are verbs nevertheless because they represent the action of the sentence.

> Blue eyes **run** in the family *(to run)*
> The family **looks** very sad *(to look)*

The verb is the most important word in a sentence. You cannot write a complete sentence and express a complete thought, without a verb.

It's important to identify verbs because they help determine the function of other verbs in a sentence. For example: the subject is the word doing the action of the verb, and the object is the word receiving the action of the verb (see *Subjects* and *Objects*).

In English

To help you learn to recognize verbs, look at the paragraph below where verbs are in *italics*.

The group of friends *entered* the café and *sat down* at a table. They *called* the waitress over, *asked* for the menu, and *ordered* some fresh coffee. They *drank* their coffee with some small cakes and pastries and then *asked* for the bill. Before they *left*, they *gave* the waitress a tip and *thanked* her. They then *left* to visit the town.

In French
Verbs are identified the same way as they are in English.

Terms used to talk about verbs:

- **Infinitive or dictionary form:** The verb form identical to the name of the verb is called an infinitive: to make, to cook, to work (see *Infinitive*). In the dictionary, verbs are listed without the *to*: make, cook, work.
- **Conjugation:** A verb is conjugated and changes form to agree with its subject: I am, he is (see *Verb Conjugation*).
- **Tense:** A verb indicates tense, which is the time (present, past, or future) of the action: I do, I did, I will do (see *Tenses*).
- **Mood:** A verb indicates mood, which is the speaker's attitude toward what he or she is saying (see *Moods*).
- **Voice:** A verb indicates voice, which is the relationship between the subject and the action of the verb (see *Active and Passive Voice*).
- **Participle:** A verb may be used to form a participle: *being → been, feeling → felt* (see *Participles*).
- **Transitive or intransitive:** A verb can be classified as transitive or intransitive depending on whether or not the verb can take a direct object (see *Objects*).

FRENCH FACT: NO CAPITALIZATION
Days of the week, months, and nationalities are not capitalized in French. Here are some examples: **lundi** *(Monday)*, **janvier** *(January)*, and **français** *(French)*.

CHAPTER 8: THE INFINITIVE

> **ILLUSTRATIVE EXAMPLE**
>
> English: ***To travel** is **to live**, **to love** is **to be** fulfilled, and **to learn** is **to grow*** endlessly in the garden of life.
>
> French: **Voyager**, c'est **vivre**, **aimer** c'est **être** épanoui, et **apprendre** c'est **grandir** sans fin dans le jardin de la vie.

The **Infinitive** form is the same as the name of the verb. For example, the French equivalent of the verb *to learn* is **étudier**.

In English
The infinitive is made up of two words: **to** + **the base form** of the verb *(to talk, to listen)*. The base form (or **Dictionary Form**) is the version of the verb you find in the dictionary *(talk, listen)*.

Although the infinitive is the most basic form of the verb, it must always be used in a sentence with another conjugated verb (see *Verb Conjugation*).

> *To explore* is thrilling.
> to explore → infinitive
> is → conjugated verb

> It is vital *to earn* some money.
> is → conjugated verb
> to earn → infinitive

> Jacqueline and André want *to eat* together.
> want → conjugated verb
> to eat → infinitive

The dictionary form of the verb *(talk, listen, cook)* is used after verbs such as *must*, *let*, and *can*.

> Marie must *go* to the hospital.
> go → dictionary form

> My father lets me *sleep* over at my friend's.
> sleep over → dictionary form

In French

The infinitive form is usually indicated by the last two or three letters of the verb called **the ending**, or *la terminaison* in French.

> manger → *to eat*
> écouter → *to listen*
> acheter → *to buy*

The infinitive form is important because it is how verbs are listed in the dictionary. The ending of the infinitive also helps show the pattern the verb will follow when it is conjugated (see *Verb Conjugation*).

> 1st conjugation → verbs ending in -er follow one pattern
> 2nd conjugation → verbs ending in -ir follow another pattern
> 3rd conjugation → verbs ending in -re follow another pattern

Consulting the Dictionary

In English, you can change the meaning of a verb by adding words like prepositions or adverbs after it.

For example, the verb *run* in Column A below changes meaning depending on the word that follows it *(into, out of, after, over)*. In French, you cannot change the meaning of a verb by adding a preposition or an adverb as in Column A. Each different meaning has its own French verb.

COLUMN A	MEANING	FRENCH
to run	to run to/in	courir
	I ran in the park	
to run into	to meet someone unexpectedly	rencontrer par hasard
	I ran into an old friend yesterday	
to run out of	to have no more of something	être à court de
	I ran out of milk	
to run after	to chase / to pursue	courir après
	the dog ran after the car	
to run over	to hit with a vehicle	écraser
	that girl was run over by a truck	

Careful – When consulting an English-French dictionary, all the examples under Column A can be found under the dictionary entry *run* (**courir**); however, you will have to search under that entry for the specific expressions *run into* (**rencontrer par hasard**), or *run over* (**écraser**), to find the correct French equivalent. Don't select the first entry under *run* and add on the French equivalent for *into*, *out of*, *after*, etc.; the result will be meaningless in French.

STUDY TIPS: THE INFINITIVE

Flashcards
• Make flashcards with the infinitive form of the French verb on one side and its English equivalent on the other. You can use a specific color for the verb cards so that you can easily tell them apart when adding more information later.
• If the verb is a reflexive verb, indicate **se** before the infinitive (see *Reflexive Verbs & Pronouns*). If the verb can be used as both a reflexive verb and a non-reflexive verb, write both.
    se laver → *to wash oneself / to take a shower*
    je me lave → *I am taking a shower*
    laver → *to wash*
    je lave mes habits → *I'm washing my clothes*
• If the verb is followed by the preposition **à** or can be part of a special construction, indicate it on the card with an example.
    penser (à + person/thing) → *to think of*
    je pense à Joséphine → *I'm thinking of Josephine*
    je pense aux voyages → *I'm thinking of trips*
 	
Practice
Follow these tips to learn the French version of English verbs. But the real practice comes when you learn to conjugate the verbs and use them in sentences.

CHAPTER 9: SUBJECTS

> **ILLUSTRATIVE EXAMPLE**
>
> English: **The teacher** guides her students through challenging lessons, while **the students** absorb knowledge and participate in classroom discussions.
>
> French: **La professeure** guide ses élèves à travers des leçons difficiles, tandis que **les élèves** absorbent les connaissances et participent aux discussions en classe.

In a sentence, the person or thing that performs the action of the verb is called the **Subject**. To find the subject of a sentence, always look for the verb first, then ask: *who?* or *what?* before the verb (see *Verbs*). The answer will be the subject, which performs the action in an active sentence, but is acted upon in a passive sentence (see *Active & Passive Voice*).

> *Marion* is cooking dinner.
> Verb: is cooking
> Who cooks dinner? Answer: Marion
> The subject refers to one person; it is singular.

> Carl's new *tech gadgets* are expensive.
> Verb: are
> What is expensive? Answer: tech gadgets
> The subject refers to more than one thing; it is plural.

If a verb has more than one subject, the subject is considered plural.

> *The cat and the dog* are playing in the garden.
> What is playing in the garden? Answer: the cat and the dog.
> The subject refers to more than one thing; it is plural.

If a sentence has more than one verb, you have to find the subject of each verb.

> My *father and brother* clean the house while my *mother* makes lunch.
> father and brother is the plural subject of clean.
> mother is the singular subject of makes.

In English
Before the verb, always ask *who?* or *what?* to find the subject. Don't assume the first word of the sentence is the subject. Subjects can be located in different places, as seen in these examples (the **subject** is in boldface and the *verb* italicized).

The **football match** *starts* at 8 pm.
After a long day of work, **Jeanne** *needs* to stretch.
My sister *is coming* to visit from London.
My cat *returned* home.

In French

The subject of a sentence is identified the same way as it is in English. It can also be located in different places in the sentence.

Careful – In English and in French it is important to find the subject of each verb to make sure that the verb form agrees with the subject (see *Verb Conjugation*).

FRENCH FACT: PLURAL OF "ŒUF" AND "ŒIL"

The plural of **œuf** *(egg)* is **œufs**, pronounced like *"urf,"* and the plural of **œil** *(eye)* is **yeux**, pronounced like *"zee-uh."* Just some of those quirky irregularities in French!

Chapter 10: Pronouns

> **ILLUSTRATIVE EXAMPLE**
>
> English: *I offered **you** a book, **you** gave **me** a watch, **he** gave **her** a dress, and **she** gave **him** a video game.*
>
> French: **Je t'**ai offert un livre, **tu m'**as donné une montre, **il lui** a donné une robe et **elle lui** a donné un jeu vidéo.

A **Pronoun** is a word used to replace one or more nouns. It can stand for a person, animal, place, thing, event, or idea. For example, instead of repeating the name *Martin* in the two sentences, you can use a pronoun to replace it in the second sentence.

> *Martin* loves traveling. *Martin* tries to travel several times a year.
> *Martin* loves traveling. *He* tries to travel several times a year.

The word that the pronoun replaces or refers to is called the **antecedent** of the pronoun. In the example above, the pronoun *he* refers to the proper noun *Martin*. *Martin* is the antecedent of the pronoun *he*.

There are different types of pronouns, each serving a different function and following different rules. Listed below are the more important types and the chapters in which they are discussed.

- **Personal pronouns:** These pronouns replace nouns referring to persons or things that were mentioned previously in the sentence. Different pronouns are used depending on the pronoun's function in the sentence.
  - *As a subject:* I speak, *they* talk, *he* listens, *she* dreams
  - *As direct object:* Mary misses *him*. Jacques enjoys *it*.
  - *As indirect object:* Manon cooked *us* dinner. Listen to *her*.
  - *As object of a preposition:* Jessica is going out with *them*.
  - *As a disjunctive:* Who is that? *Me*.

- **Reflexive pronouns:** These pronouns refer back to the subject of the sentence.
  > You washed *yourself*.
  > She cut *herself* with a knife.
  > Laurent taught *himself* to speak French.

- **Interrogative pronouns:** These pronouns are used to ask questions.

What is this?
What do they want?

- **Demonstrative pronouns:** These pronouns are used to refer to persons or things.
    That (one) is better.
    These (ones) are delicious.

- **Possessive pronouns:** These pronouns are used to indicate possession.
    Whose phone is that? It's *hers*.

- **Relative pronouns:** These pronouns are used to introduce relative clauses.
    The woman *who* was here earlier is French.
    Where is the box *where* you store photos?

- **Indefinite pronouns:** These pronouns are used to refer to unidentified persons or things.
    One cannot think like that.
    Something isn't right.

In English
Each type of pronoun follows a different set of rules.

In French
As in English, in French, each type of pronoun follows a different set of rules and usually agree in gender and number with their antecedent (see *Gender and Number*).

FRENCH FACT: THE TWO FORMS OF "YOU"
In French, there are two forms of *you*: **tu** and **vous**. **Tu** is used for informal situations or when addressing someone familiar, like a friend or family member, while **vous** is used to address someone in formal situations (a politician, a president, a professor) or when addressing multiple people.

Chapter 11: Subject Pronouns

> **ILLUSTRATIVE EXAMPLE**
>
> <u>English:</u> **He** plays the piano beautifully, while **she** sings with a voice like an angel. Together, **they** create music that enchants everyone who hears it.
>
> <u>French:</u> **Il** joue du piano magnifiquement, tandis qu'**elle** chante avec une voix d'ange. Ensemble, **ils** créent une musique qui enchante tous ceux qui l'entendent.

A **Subject Pronoun** is a word that replaces a noun and acts as the subject of a verb (see *Subjects*).

> *She* studied while *he* took a nap.
> Who studied? Answer: she.
> She is the subject of the verb studied.
> Who took a nap? Answer: he.
> He is the subject of the verb took a nap.

Pronouns that refer to people or things are divided into three groups: 1st, 2nd, and 3rd person. Here, **Person** is a grammatical term and can refer to any noun, not just a human.

In English
Here is a list of English subject pronouns grouped according to the person to which they belong.

1st person
I → the person speaking → singular
we → the person speaking plus others → plural
> *Marcus and I* want to go out tonight. *We* are going to a bar.

2nd person
you → the person or persons spoken to → singular or plural
> Jacques, can *you* make French pastries?
> Jacques, Manon, and Anaïs, can *you* make French pastries?

3rd person
he, she, it → the person or object spoken about → singular
they → the persons or objects spoken about → plural
> Where is *my wallet*? *It* is on your desk.
> *Marcus and Anna* are in town. *They* want to meet with us.

In French

French subject pronouns are also grouped by person. They are presented in the following order:

SINGULAR		
1st PERSON	*I*	je
2nd PERSON	*you*	tu
3rd PERSON	*he, she, it*	il, elle, il or elle, on
PLURAL		
1st PERSON	*we*	nous, on
2nd PERSON	*you*	vous
3rd PERSON	*they*	ils, elles

As you can see, some English subject pronouns have more than one equivalent in French: *you* (**tu** or **vous**), *it* (**il** or **elle**), *we* (**nous** or **on**), and *they* (**ils** or **elles**). Let's look at each of these pronouns.

"You" (2nd Person Singular & Plural)

    tu   (2nd person familiar singular) or
    vous (2nd person formal to address one or more persons)
             (2nd person familiar plural)

In English

The subject pronoun *you* is used when you are speaking to one person or more.

    Jacques, are *you* going to the party?
    Jacques, Marie, Marcus, are *you* going to the party?

The same pronoun *you* is used to address the President of the United States or your dog.

    How are *you*, Mr. President?
    You are such a good boy, Spot!

In French
When you are speaking to one person, there are two forms of *you* in French. The form you use will depend on the person you address and whether you are on familiar terms.

- When speaking to a child, an animal, a family member, a friend, or anyone with whom you are on familiar terms, use the **familiar form** → **tu** (2nd person singular).
    *Dad, at what time are **you** leaving? you* → **tu**
    Papa, à quelle heure pars-**tu** ?

- When speaking to a person with whom you are not on familiar terms, use the formal form → **vous** (2nd person plural). Note that this formal form is used to address *one person*.
    *Ms. Duchemin, how are **you** today? you* → **vous**
    Mademoiselle Duchemin, comment allez-**vous** aujourd'hui ?

If you're speaking to an adult and aren't sure which form to use, it is preferable to use **vous**.

- When speaking to more than one person - whether you are on familiar terms with them or not - there is only one form → **vous** (2nd person plural).
    *Jacques and Muriel, are **you** going to be there? you* → **vous**
    Jacques et Muriel, est-ce que **vous** y serez ?

    *Mr. and Mrs. Arnaud, how are **you** today? you* → **vous**
    Monsieur et Madame Arnaud, comment allez-**vous** aujourd'hui ?

"It" (3rd Person Singular)

il (3rd person singular masculine) or
elle (3rd person singular feminine)

In English
The subject pronoun *it* is used whenever you are speaking about one thing.

Have you seen my phone? *It* is on the kitchen counter.

In French
The subject pronoun used depends on the gender of its **antecedent**, which is the

noun it replaces.

- **Masculine antecedent → il**
    Où est mon téléphone portable? **Il** est sur la table de la cuisine.
    - téléphone portable → masc. sing. antecedent
    - il → masc. sing. pronoun

    Where is my phone? *It* is on the kitchen counter.

- **Feminine antecedent → elle**
    Voici la nouvelle télévision. **Elle** est belle, n'est-ce pas ?
    - télévision → fem. sing. antecedent
    - elle → fem. sing. pronoun

    Here's the new television. *It's* beautiful, isn't it?

"We" (1st Person Plural)

nous   (1st person plural) or
on   (3rd person singular)

In English
The subject pronoun *we* is used when you are speaking about yourself and one or more other persons.

Jacques and I are colleagues; *we* work for the same company.
I am leaving with my co-workers; *we* are going to the party together.

In French
The subject pronoun is either the 1st person plural **nous** or, mainly in spoken French, the 3rd person singular **on**. If you use **nous**, the verb will be in the 1st person plural form. If you use **on**, the verb will be in the 3rd person singular form (see *Verb Conjugation*).

We have a lot of work.
   Nous avons beaucoup de travail. → 1st person plural
   On a beaucoup de travail. → 3rd person singular

Remember, no matter what is **on**'s equivalent in English, the French verb is always in the 3rd person singular form.

"They" (3rd Person Plural)

    ils   (3rd person plural masculine) or
    elles   (3rd person plural feminine)

In English
The subject pronoun *they* is used when you are speaking about more than one person or thing.

    Marion and Joachim are co-workers; *they* work together.
    I can't find my keys. Do you know where *they* are?

In French
The subject pronoun used depends on the gender of its **antecedent**, that is, the noun it replaces.

- **Masculine antecedent → ils**

    Où sont les chiens ? **Ils** ne sont pas dans le jardin.
        chiens → masc. pl. antecedent
        ils → masc. pl. pronoun
    *Where are the dogs? **They** are not in the garden.*

    Carl et Joachim sont collègues ; **ils** travaillent pour la même société.
        Carl et Joachim → 2 masc. sing. antecedents
        ils → masc. pl. pronoun
    *Carl and Joachim are colleagues; **they** work for the same company.*

    Où as-tu mis les légumes ? **Ils** sont dans le frigo.
        légumes → masc. pl. antecedent
        ils → masc. pl. pronoun
    *Where did you put the vegetables? **They** are in the fridge.*

- **Feminine antecedent → elles**

    À quelle heure sont les réunions ? **Elles** sont à quinze et seize heures.
        réunions → fem. pl. antecedent
        elles → fem. pl. pronoun
    *At what time are the meetings? **They** are at 3pm and 4pm.*

    Carole et Manon quittent demain ; **elles** vont au Cambodge.
        Carole et Manon → 2 fem. sing. antecedents
        elles → fem. pl. pronoun
    *Carole and Manon are leaving tomorrow; **they** are going to Cambodia.*

Je ne trouve pas les glaces. **Elles** ne sont pas dans le frigo ?
glaces → fem. pl. antecedent
elles → fem. pl. pronoun
*I can't find the ice creams. Are **they** not in the fridge?*

STUDY TIPS: SUBJECT PRONOUNS
Flashcards
Create a flashcard for each subject pronoun (1st, 2nd, and 3rd person singular and plural). Then add on the other forms of the pronoun as you learn them.

SINGULAR		
1st PERSON	*I*	je
2nd PERSON	*you*	tu
3rd PERSON	*he, she, it*	il, elle, on
PLURAL		
1st PERSON	*we*	nous
2nd PERSON	*you*	vous
3rd PERSON	*they*	ils, elles

Practice
You will practice subject pronouns when you'll practice conjugating verbs.

Chapter 12: Verb Conjugation

> **ILLUSTRATIVE EXAMPLE**
>
> English: *As the flowers **bloom** in spring, we **forget** the winter, the children **will start playing** in the garden and the birds **will sing**.*
>
> French: *Alors que les fleurs **fleurissent** au printemps, on **oublie** l'hiver, les enfants **commenceront** à jouer dans le jardin et les oiseaux **chanteront**.*

A **Verb Conjugation** is a list of the six possible forms of a verb for a specific tense. Each form matches one of the subject pronouns (see *Tenses*).

> I am
> you are (one person)
> he, she, it is
> we are
> you are (two+ persons)
> they are

Different tenses have different verb forms, but conjugation works the same for each tense. In this chapter, all our examples are in the present tense (see *The Present Tense*).

In English

The verb *to be* in English changes the most, with three forms: *am*, *are*, and *is*. (The initial vowel is often replaced by an apostrophe: *I'm, you're, he's*). Most other English verbs, like *to play*, only have two forms: *play, plays*.

SINGULAR	
1st PERSON	I play
2nd PERSON	you play
3rd PERSON	he, she, it plays
PLURAL	
1st PERSON	we play
2nd PERSON	you play
3rd PERSON	they play

Because English verbs change so little, you don't need to learn how to "conjugate" them, or list all their forms. For most verbs, you just add an *s* for the third person singular.

In French

Unlike in English, in French verb forms change from one person to the next. So, when you learn a new French verb, you also need to learn how to conjugate it. First, you must find out if the verb is regular or irregular.

- Verbs that follow a set pattern are called **Regular Verbs**. You only need to memorize one example, and then you can apply the same pattern to other verbs in that group.
- Verbs that do not follow a set pattern are called **Irregular Verbs.** These verbs must be memorized one by one. Unfortunately, the most commonly used French verbs are irregular.

The forms of a verb, whether regular or irregular, are memorized with subject pronouns and the verb forms that agree with them (see *Subject Pronouns*). This list of subject pronouns and verb forms is called the conjugation of the verb (**la conjugaison**).

Choosing the Proper Person

Below is the conjugation of the regular verb **manger** *(to eat)*. Each of the six subjects has its own ending. Different pronouns belonging to the same person share the same verb form. For example, the 3rd person singular pronouns **il, elle,** and **on** all use the verb form **mange**.

SINGULAR		
1st PERSON	je mange	*I eat*
2nd PERSON	tu manges	*you eat*
3rd PERSON	il, elle, on mange	*he, she, it eats*
PLURAL		
1st PERSON	nous mangeons	*we eat*
2nd PERSON	vous mangez	*you eat*
3rd PERSON	ils, elles mangent	*they eat*

To choose the proper verb form, you must first identify the person (1st, 2nd, or 3rd) and the number (singular or plural) of the subject.

1st Person Singular – The subject is always je (*I*):

Je suis toujours fatiguée le matin.
I am always tired in the morning.

2nd Person Singular – The subject is always tu (informal *you*):

Jacques, **tu** as tout mangé !
*Jacques, **you** ate everything!*

3rd Person Singular – The subject can be expressed in one of four ways:

1. A proper noun:

Martin mange beaucoup.
Martin eats a lot.
  Martin = masc. sing. → il *(he)*

Angélique est grande.
Angélique is tall.
  Angélique = fem. sing. → elle *(she)*

In both sentences the proper noun could be replaced by the pronoun **she** (*elle → fem.*) or **he** (*il → masc.*), so you must use the 3rd person singular form of the verb.

2. A singular common noun:

L'homme mange beaucoup.
The man eats a lot.
  L'homme = masc. sing. → il *(he)*

L'autruche court vite.
The ostrich runs fast.
  L'autruche = fem. sing. → elle *(it)*

In both sentences the proper noun could be replaced by the pronoun **he** *(il*

→ *masc.*) or **it** *(elle → fem.)*, so you must use the 3rd person singular form of the verb.

3. The 3rd person singular masculine pronoun il *(he, it)* or the 3rd person singular feminine pronoun elle *(she, it)*:

Fanny aime la mode. **Elle** fait beaucoup de shopping.
Fanny likes fashion. ***She*** *does a lot of shopping.*
Fanny / elle = fem. sing.

J'ai lu ce livre. **Il** est très bien écrit.
I read this book. ***It*** *is very well written.*
Ce livre / il = masc. sing.

Joachim adore les échecs. **Il** est un champion !
Joachim loves chess. ***He's*** *a champion!*
Joachim / il = masc. sing.

J'ai acheté cette boîte. **Elle** est jolie, n'est-ce pas ?
I bought this box. ***It's*** *beautiful, isn't it?*
Cette boîte / elle = fem. sing.

4. The 3rd person singular pronoun on *(we)*:

On s'amuse bien ensemble.
We *have fun together.*
On = 3rd person sing.

1st Person Plural – The subject can be expressed in one of two ways:

1. A multiple subject in which the speaker is included:

Marion, Jacques et moi partons ensemble.
Marion, Jacques and I *are leaving together.*
Marion, Jacques et moi = nous

The subject, *Marion, Jacques and I* could be replaced by the pronoun **we**, so you must use the 1st person plural form of the verb.

2. The first person plural pronoun nous *(we)*:

Nous partons ensemble.
We are leaving together.

2nd Person Plural – The subject is always vous *(you)*:

Monsieur et Madame Arnaud, **vous** formez un beau couple.
*Mr. and Mrs. Arnaud, **you** make a great couple.*

Madame Arnaud, **vous** avez une belle tenue !
*Mrs. Arnaud, **you** have a beautiful outfit!*

3rd Person Plural – The subject can be expressed in one of three ways:

1. A plural noun:

Les enfants jouent ensemble.
***The children** are playing together.*
    Les enfants = masc. pl. → ils *(they)*

2. Two or more proper or common nouns:

Manon et Anaïs sont meilleures amies.
***Manon and Anaïs** are best friends.*
    Manon et Anaïs = fem. + fem. → elles *(they)*

Marcus et Carole forment un beau couple.
***Marcus and Carole** make a beautiful couple.*
    Marcus et Carole = masc. + fem. → ils *(they)*

3. The 3rd person plural masculine pronoun ils *(they)* or the 3rd person plural feminine pronoun elles *(they)*

Maxime et Arnaud travaillent ensemble. **Ils** sont collègues.
***Maxime and Arnaux** work together. **They** are colleagues.*
    Maxime et Arnaud = masc. + masc. → ils *(they)*

Vous avez vu **les oiseaux** ? **Ils** sont fascinants !
*Did you see **the birds**? **They** are fascinating!*
    Les oiseaux / ils = masc. pl.

Marion et Camille voyagent ensemble. **Elles** vont en Allemagne.

Marion and Camille *are traveling together. They are going to Germany.*
Marion et Camille = fem. + fem. → elles *(they)*

J'ai acheté des nouvelles **assiettes**. **Elles** sont belles.
*I bought new **plates**. **They** are beautiful.*
Les assiettes / elles = fem. pl.

How to Conjugate a Verb

A French verb, whether regular or irregular, is composed of two parts:

1. The stem or root (la racine) is found by dropping the last two letters from the infinitive (see *The Inifinitive*).

INFINITIVE	STEM
manger	mang-
réussir	réuss-
rendre	rend-

The stem of regular verbs usually remains the same throughout a conjugation. You will have to memorize the changes in the stem of irregular verbs.

2. The ending, (la terminaison) changes for each person in the conjugation of regular and irregular verbs.

Regular verbs are divided into three **groups**, also called **conjugations**. They are identified by the last two letters of the infinitive ending of the verb.

1st GROUP	2nd GROUP	3rd GROUP
-er	-ir	-re

Each of the three verb groups has its own set of endings for each tense (see *Tenses*). By memorizing the conjugation of one sample verb for each tense in each group, you can learn to conjugate other irregular verbs in that group.

To understand how to conjugate a regular verb, let's look at the 1st group of verbs (those ending in **-er**). Examples are **regarder** *(to look)* and **marcher** *(to walk)*, which follow the same pattern as **manger** *(to eat)* that we saw earlier.

1. Identify the group of the verb by its infinitive ending:
   regarder → 1st conjugation group
   marcher

2. Find the verb stem by removing the infinitive ending:
   regard-
   march-

3. Add the ending that agrees with the subject:

Je regard**e**	Je march**e**
Tu regard**es**	Tu march**es**
Il/Elle/On regard**e**	Il/Elle/On march**e**
Nous regard**ons**	Nous march**ons**
Vous regard**ez**	Vous march**ez**
Ils/Elles regard**ent**	Ils/Elles march**ent**

The endings of regular verbs from the other groups are different, but the process of conjugation is the same. Just follow the three steps above.

When you learn irregular verbs, you'll normally get the full list of their forms so you can memorize them individually. It's important to do this because the most common French verbs are irregular: **être** *(to be)*, **avoir** *(to have)*, **aller** *(to go)*, **faire** *(to make)*.

Careful – French verb forms are often pronounced the same way, but written differently (for instance, *parle, parles, parlent*). The only way to write the proper ending of a verb is to identify its subject.

STUDY TIPS: VERB CONJUGATIONS

- **Regular -er verbs**

    Pattern - As in all regular verbs, the stem usually remains the same throughout the conjugation; only the endings change according to the subject.

    Look at conjugation of **chanter** *(to sing)*:

Je chant**e**	Nous chant**ons**
Tu chant**es**	Vous chant**ez**
Il/Elle/On chant**e**	Ils/Elles chant**ent**

    Regular -er verbs follow the same pattern: most forms sound the same. When you learn new verbs and conjugations, check if they fit this pattern. If they do, it will be easier to remember.

    Practice
    1. When learning verb conjugations, write the different forms repeatedly until you can do it without looking at the conjugation. Remember, many forms sound the same, so link the spelling of each ending with its subject.
    2. Apply the pattern you learned to another regular -**er** verb.
    3. Create your own sentences using the different forms of regular -**er** verbs.
    4. Practice using the various forms out of order so you don't need to recite the whole conjugation when speaking.
    5. Only do exercises after understanding the explanations and examples. Don't look at the answers while doing exercises; treat them as a self-test. After finishing, use a colored pen to correct your mistakes so they stand out during review.

    Flashcards
    Take out the flashcards you created to learn the meaning of verbs and add the following information on the French side:

    - Indicate that the verb is regular. For example:

        aimer (reg.)   to love

    - Indicate any irregularity in the stem

        manger   to eat
        nous mangeons   we eat

- **Regular -ir verbs**

    Pattern - As in all regular verbs, the stem usually remains the same throughout the conjugation; only the endings change according to the subject.

    Look at conjugation of **choisir** *(to choose)*:

Je choisi**s**	Nous choisi**ssons**
Tu choisi**s**	Vous choisi**ssez**
Il/Elle/On choisi**t**	Ils/Elles choisi**ssent**

    Regular **-ir** verbs follow a simple pattern: all the singular forms on the left sound the same, and all the plural forms on the right have an "ss" in spelling and an "s" sound in pronunciation.

    When you're learning new verb conjugations, compare them to ones you already know. This helps you see what's similar and different, making it easier to focus on the forms you need to learn and to tell the conjugations apart. For regular **-ir** verbs, check how their endings compare to those of regular **-er** verbs with the same subjects.

    Practice and flashcards
    See suggestions for regular **-er** verbs on the previous page.

- **Regular -re verbs**

    Pattern - As in all regular verbs, the stem usually remains the same throughout the conjugation; only the endings change according to the subject.

    Look at conjugation of **vendre** *(to sell)*:

Je vend**s**	Nous vend**ons**
Tu vend**s**	Vous vend**ez**
Il/Elle/On vend	Ils/Elles vend**ent**

    Regular **-re** verbs follow a simple pattern: all the singular forms on the left sound the same, and all the plural forms on the right have a "d" sound in the pronunciation.

- **Irregular verbs**

    Pattern – As in all irregular verbs, the stem as well as the endings can change throughout out the conjugation.

    Start by looking for a pattern within the conjugation of the irregular verb.

    - **Stem:** look for similarities in the various forms.
    - **Endings:** look for similarities with verbs you have already learned.

    For example, let's look at the irregular verb **écrire** *(to write)*:

    | J'écris | Nous écriv**ons** |
    | Tu écris | Vous écriv**ez** |
    | Il/Elle/On écrit | Ils/Elles écriv**ent** |

    - **Stem:** there is a boot pattern similar to regular **-er** verbs. There is also a vertical pattern similar to regular **-ir** verbs.
        - All the stems start with **écri-**
        - All the plural stems have a "v"

    - **Endings:** although the endings change, there are similarities with the endings of regular verbs.
        - The singular forms have the same endings as regular **-ir** verbs.
        - The plural forms have the same endings as regular **-er** verbs.

    Careful – There are verbs that do not fit in either the boot or vertical pattern. You will have to look for a pattern if there is one.

    Practice and flashcards
    See suggestions for regular **-er** verbs above. On the flash cards, be sure to indicate when the verb is irregular by adding (irreg.) next to it.

CHAPTER 13: AUXILIARY VERBS

> **ILLUSTRATIVE EXAMPLE**
>
> English: *They **are going** to the park with their friends and **have brought** their picnic basket, blankets, and games to enjoy.*
>
> French: Ils vont au parc avec leurs amis et **ont apporté** leur panier de pique-nique, des couvertures et des jeux pour s'amuser.

A verb is called an **Auxiliary Verb** or **Helping Verb** when it helps another verb (the **Main Verb**) form its tenses.

> She **has been** working for a month.
>   has → auxiliary verb
>   been → auxiliary verb
>   working → main verb

In English

There are three main auxiliary verbs: **have**, **be**, and **do**. Additionally, we use other words like **will**, **would**, **may**, **must**, **can**, and **could** to change the tense and meaning of the main verb.

Auxiliaries are used primarily to indicate the tense of the main verb (present, past, future – see *Tenses*).

Marc *is working* in cryptocurrency *auxiliary: to be*	Present
Marc *has worked* in cryptocurrency *auxiliary: to have*	Past
Marc *will work* in cryptocurrency *auxiliary: to be*	Future

The verb *to do* helps to formulate questions and make negative sentences (see *Declarative and Interrogative Sentences* and *Affirmative and Negative Sentences*).

Does Marc work in cryptocurrency?	Interrogative sentence
Marc *does not* work in cryptocurrency	Negative sentence

In French

There are only two auxiliary verbs: **avoir** *(to have)* and **être** *(to be)*. They are used to change the tense of the main verb.

The English auxiliary verbs like **do, does, did, will,** or **would,** do not exist in French. Instead, their meanings are shown by different structures or forms of the main verb. You can learn more about this in the chapters on different tenses.

The verbs **avoir** and **être** are irregular verbs whose conjugations must be memorized. They're important verbs because they serve both as **auxiliary verbs** and **main verbs**.

J'ai un chat	**avoir** *(to have)*	Main verb
I have a cat		
J'ai mangé du gâteau	**avoir** *(to have)*	Auxiliary
I ate some cake	to eat	Main verb
Je suis français	**être** *(to be)*	Main verb
I am French		
Je suis allée à la plage	**être** *(to be)*	Auxiliary
I went to the beach	to go	Main verb

A verb tense composed of an auxiliary verb + a main verb is called a **compound tense**, as opposed to a **simple tense** that is a tense composed of only the main verb.

> Je **dors**. → *I sleep.*
>   dors → simple tense, present of dormir
>
> **J'ai dormi.** → *I have slept.*
>   ai → auxiliary verb
>   dormi → main verb
>   ai + dormi → compound tense, past tense of dormir

Auxiliary Verbs to Indicate Tense

To form all compound tenses in French, we use either **avoir** or **être** as auxiliary verbs. The auxiliary verb is conjugated in different tenses, and we add the past participle of the main verb. Here are some examples. The first sentence of each pair uses **avoir** as the auxiliary verb (for example: **voir** - *to see*), and the second sentence uses **être** as the auxiliary verb.

- **Passé composé (present perfect)** – Present of **avoir** or **être** + past participle of main verb (see *The Past Tense*). Notice that there are two possible English equivalents.

> Marie **a vu** le film.
> *Marie **saw (has seen)** the film.*
>
> Martin **est allé** en France.
> *Martin **went (has been)** to France.*

- **Plus-que-parfait (past perfect)** – Imperfect of **avoir** or **être** + past participle of main verb (see *The Past Perfect Tense*).

   > Marie **avait vu** le film.
   > *Marie **had seen** the film.*
   >
   > Martin **était allé** en France.
   > *Martin **had been** to France.*

- **Futur antérieur (future perfect)** – Future of **avoir** or **être** + past participle of main verb (see *The Future Perfect Tense*).

   > Marie **aura vu** le film.
   > *Marie **will have seen** the film.*
   >
   > Martin **sera allé** en France.
   > *Martin **will have been** to France.*

- **Conditionnel passé (past conditional)** – Conditional of **avoir** or **être** + past participle of main verb (see *The Conditional*).

   > Marie **aurait vu** le film.
   > *Marie **would have seen** the film.*
   >
   > Martin **serait allé** en France.
   > *Martin **would have been** to France.*

You will learn other compound tenses as your study of French progresses.

FRENCH FACT: LONGEST WORD
The longest French word in the dictionary is **anticonstitutionnellement**, meaning unconstitutionally, made up of twenty-five letters.

CHAPTER 14: AFFIRMATIVE AND NEGATIVE SENTENCES

> **ILLUSTRATIVE EXAMPLE**
>
> English: ***She always smiles*** *at everyone, but* ***he never talks*** *to strangers, creating a balance of friendliness and introversion in their interactions.*
>
> French: **Elle sourit toujours** à tout le monde, mais **il ne parle jamais** aux étrangers, créant un équilibre entre la convivialité et l'introversion dans leurs interactions.

A sentence can be classified according to whether it states that something is true or that something is not true.

An **Affirmative Sentence** is a sentence that states a positive fact.

> Belgium *is* part of the European Union.
> Béatrice *will* become a lawyer.
> He *enjoyed* his trip to Paris.

A **Negative Sentence** is a sentence that states a fact that is denied.

> Germany *is not* part of Asia.
> Carl *will not* work as a doctor.
> She *did not* like Bali.

In English
An affirmative sentence can be made negative in one or two ways:

1. By adding ***not*** after an auxiliary verb or an auxiliary word (see *Auxiliary Verbs*).

AFFIRMATIVE	NEGATIVE
She is an employee.	She is *not* an employee.
You can do it.	You *cannot* do it.
He will succeed.	He will *not* succeed.

The word *not* is often attached to the auxiliary and the letter "o" is replaced by an apostrophe; this is called a **contraction**: *is not* → *isn't*; *cannot* → *can't*; *will not* → *won't*.

2. By adding the auxiliary verb **do, does,** or **did + not,** and giving the dictionary form of the main verb.

AFFIRMATIVE	NEGATIVE
She works a lot.	She *does not* work a lot.
They sing well.	They *don't* sing well.
The plane landed.	The plane *did not* land.

Frequently, *do, does,* or *did* is contracted with *not*: *do not* → *don't*; *does not* → *doesn't*; *did not* → *didn't*.

In French
An affirmative sentence is made negative by putting **ne** (or **n'** before a vowel) right after the subject and the negative **pas** *(not)* after the conjugated verb.

AFFIRMATIVE	NEGATIVE
Ils travaillent beaucoup.	Ils **ne** travaillent **pas** beaucoup. → travaillent: conjugated verb
They work a lot.	*They **don't** work a lot.*
Myriam danse bien.	Myriam **ne** danse **pas** bien. → danse: conjugated verb
Myriam dances well.	*Myriam **doesn't** dance well.*
La maison est terminée.	La maison **n'**est **pas** terminée. → est: conjugated verb
The house is finished.	*The house is **not** finished.*

Careful – Remember that there is no equivalent for the auxiliary words *do, does, did* in French. Do not try to include them in negative sentences.

Negative Words

In English and in French there are other negative words besides *not* (**ne... pas**).

In English
There are two types of negative words: those used in positive sentences and their equivalents used in negative sentences. Here are the most common negative words.

NEGATIVE WORDS Affirmative Sentences	NEGATIVE WORDS Negative Sentences
never	ever
no longer	any longer
no more	anymore
nobody	anybody
no one	anyone
nothing	anything

Let's look at some examples:

- **never, ever**
    I *never* drive at night.
    I don't *ever* drive at night.

- **no longer (no more), any longer (anymore)**
    I will *no longer* contact him.
    I won't contact him *anymore*.

- **nobody (no one), anybody (anyone)**
    There was *no one* at the shop.
    There wasn't *anybody* at the shop.

- **nothing, anything**
    I brought *nothing* with me.
    I didn't bring *anything* with me.

In French

Unlike in English, there is only one set of negative words in French. The most commons are: **jamais** *(never, ever)*, **plus** *(no longer, no more, any longer, anymore)*, **personne** *(nobody, anybody)*, and **rien** *(nothing, anything)*.

In most cases, the placement of these negative words is the same as the negative word **pas** → after the conjugated verb.

- *Never, ever* → **ne... jamais**
    Je **ne** mets **jamais** de chaussettes quand je dors.
    *I **never** wear socks when I sleep.*
    *I **don't ever** wear socks when I sleep.*

- *No longer, no more, any longer, anymore* → **ne... plus**
    Il **ne** sait **plus** parler français.
    *He **no longer** knows how to speak French.*
    *He doesn't know how to speak French **anymore**.*

- *Nobody, anybody* (**personne**) and *nothing, anything* (**rien**)

    Subject of a sentence → **personne/rien + ne**
        Personne ne se lève tôt le matin.
        No one gets up early in the morning.

        Rien n'est fait.
        ***Nothing** is done.*

    Object of a verb in a simple tense → **ne... personne/rien**
        Elle **ne** mange **rien**.
        *She eats **nothing**.*
        *She doesn't eat **anything**.*

        Il **n'y** a **personne** à la maison.
        *There's **no one** home.*
        *There isn't **anyone** home.*

    Rien object of a verb in a compound tense → **ne** + auxiliary verb + **rien** + past participle
        Il **n'a rien** mangé.
        *He ate **nothing**.*
        *He didn't eat **anything**.*

    Personne object of a verb in a compound tense → **ne** + auxiliary verb + past participle + **personne**
        Il **n'y** avait **personne**, c'était vide.
        *There was **no one**, it was empty.*
        *There wasn't **anyone**, it was empty.*

The above is an introduction to negative words and where to place them.

FRENCH FACT: OMITTING "NE"
In casual spoken French, the negative particle **ne** often disappears, so **je ne sais pas** *(I don't know)* becomes **je sais pas**.

Chapter 15: Declarative and Interrogative Sentences

> **ILLUSTRATIVE EXAMPLE**
>
> English: ***The sun sets*** *over the horizon, casting a golden glow.* ***Will*** *tomorrow* ***be*** *just as lovely?*
>
> French: **Le soleil se couche** à l'horizon, projetant une lueur dorée. Demain **sera-t-il** aussi charmant ?

A sentence can be classified as to whether it is making a statement or asking a question.

A **Declarative Sentence** is a sentence that makes a statement.

The Soviet Union ended in 1991.

An **Interrogative Sentence** is a sentence that asks a question.

Did the Soviet Union end in 1991?

In written language, an interrogative sentence always ends with a question mark.

In English
A declarative sentence can be changed into an interrogative sentence in two ways:

1. By adding the auxiliary verb **do, does**, or **did** before the subject and using the dictionary form of the main verb:

DECLARATIVE SENTENCES	INTERROGATIVE SENTENCES
Marion enjoyed the dinner you cooked.	*Did Marion* enjoy the dinner you cooked?
Jacques and Marcus work together.	*Do Jacques and Marcus* work together?
He traveled to Indonesia.	*Did he* travel to Indonesia?

2. By inverting the normal word order of subject + verb to verb + subject. This inversion only works by using auxiliary verbs or auxiliary words (see *Auxiliary Verbs*).

DECLARATIVE SENTENCES	INTERROGATIVE SENTENCES
Julie's daughter is at school.	*Is Julie's daughter* at school?
They have received an invitation.	*Have they* received an invitation?
Carl is leaving with her.	*Is Carl* leaving with her?

In French
A declarative sentence can be changed into an interrogative sentence in two ways:

1. By adding the expression **est-ce que** before the complete declarative sentence:

> **Est-ce qu'il** peut partir maintenant ?
>   He can leave now
>   complete declarative sentence
> ***Can he** leave now?*

> **Est-ce que Marc** rentre ce soir ?
>   Marc comes home tonight
>   complete declarative sentence
> ***Is Marc** coming home tonight?*

2. By using the **inversion form**:

When the subject is a pronoun (except for the subject pronoun **je** which can only use the expression **est-ce que**), invert the verb and pronoun subject.

> **Tu rentres** à la maison ce soir.
> **Rentres-tu** à la maison ce soir ?
> ***You are coming** home tonight.*
> ***Are you coming** home tonight?*

When the subject is a noun, construct the question as follows:

- State the noun subject.
- State the verb and, when writing, add a hyphen.
- State the subject pronoun that corresponds to the gender and number of the subject.

Let's look at a few examples:

> **Manon** est-**elle** au bureau ?
> (word-for-word: *Manon is she at the office?*)
>   Noun subject: Manon → fem. sing. → pronoun fem. sing. → **elle**
> ***Is Manon** at the office?*

Les livres sont-**ils** sur l'étagère ?
(word-for-word: *the books are they on the shelf?*)
    Noun subject: **les livres** → masc. pl. → pronoun masc. pl. → **ils**
Are the books on the shelf?

Julien et Camille sont-**ils** partis ?
(word-for-word: *Julien and Camille are they gone?*)
    Two noun subjects: **Julien** → masc. sing. and **Camille** → fem. sing. → pronoun masc. pl. → **ils**
Are Julien and Camille gone?

When a verb ending with a vowel in the 3rd person singular is inverted, **-t-** is added between the verb and the subject pronoun to facilitate pronunciation.

    Marion **mange-t-elle** à la maison ce soir ?
    ***Is** Marion **eating** at home tonight?*

    Martin **aime-t-il** le poisson ?
    ***Does** Martin **like** fish?*

Careful – When *do*, *does*, or *did* are used as auxiliaries, do not translate them to French. Just like the expression **est-ce que**, they are used to turn the complete sentence that follows into a question.

Tag Questions

In both English and French, when you want a yes-or-no answer, you can turn a statement into a question by adding a short phrase at the end. This short phrase is called a **tag**.

In English
There are many different tags to use, depending on the tense of the verb and whether the statement is positive or negative. Affirmative statements use negative tags, and negative statements use affirmative tags (see *Affirmative and Negative Sentences*).

    Marie and Jean *work* together, *don't they?*
    Marie and Jean *don't work* together, *do they?*

In French
There is only one tag, which is **n'est-ce pas ?** You can add it to any statement to

make it a yes-or-no question.

> Marie et Jean travaillent ensemble, **n'est-ce pas ?**
> *Marie and Jean work together, **don't they?***

> Marie et Jean ne travaillent pas ensemble, **n'est-ce pas ?**
> *Marie and Jean don't work together, **do they?***

FRENCH FACT: POETIC FREEDOM
French poets and writers often take liberties with grammar and structure for artistic effect, which can be confusing for learners.

Chapter 16: Tenses

> **ILLUSTRATIVE EXAMPLE**
>
> English: *Yesterday, she **danced** gracefully while she **dances** passionately today, and she **will dance** joyfully tomorrow, showcasing her love for movement.*
>
> French: *Hier, elle **dansait** gracieusement tandis qu'elle **danse** passionnément aujourd'hui, et elle **dansera** joyeusement demain, démontrant son amour pour le mouvement.*

The **Tense** of a verb indicates when the action happens: now *(present)*, before *(past)*, or later *(future)*. The word *tense* comes from the French word **temps**, which means time.

I am changing.	Present
I changed.	Past
I will change.	Future

As you can see in the examples above, you can indicate when the action takes place by simply changing the tense of the verb, like: *I'm changing, I changed,* or *I will change*.

Tenses can be classified as **simple** or **compound**. A **simple tense** has just one verb form, like *I changed*. A **compound tense** has an auxiliary verb + the main verb, like *I am changing* or *she has been changing* (see *Auxiliary Verbs*).

In this section, we will only consider tenses of the **indicative mood** (see *Moods*).

In English
Listed below are the main tenses of the indicative mood whose equivalents you will encounter in French.

PRESENT	
I eat	Present
I do eat	Present Emphatic
I am eating	Present Progressive
PAST	

I ate	Simple Past
I did eat	Past Emphatic
I have eaten	Present Perfect
I had eaten	Past Perfect
I was eating	Past Progressive
FUTURE	
I will eat	Future
I will have eaten	Future Perfect

As you can see, there are only two simple tenses: **present** and **simple past**; all the other tenses are compound tenses.

In French

Listed below are the main tenses of the indicative mood that you will encounter in French.

PRESENT		
Je mange	*I eat* *I am eating* *I do eat*	Présent *(Present)*
PAST		
J'ai mangé	*I ate* *I have eaten* *I did eat*	Passé Composé *(Present Perfect)*
Je mangeais	*I was eating* *I used to eat*	Imparfait *(Imperfect)*
J'avais mangé	*I had eaten*	Plus-que-Parfait *(Past Perfect)*
FUTURE		
Je mangerai	*I will eat*	Futur *(Future)*
J'aurais mangé	*I will have eaten*	Futur Antérieur *(Future Perfect)*

French has more simple tenses than English, such as the present, imperfect, and future. French compound tenses are formed with the auxiliary verbs **avoir** *(to have)* or **être** *(to be)* + the past participle of the main verb. For example, the verb **manger** *(to eat)* uses **avoir** to form its compound tenses.

This handbook covers the various tenses and their usage in separate chapters: *The Present Tense, The Past Tense, The Past Perfect Tense, The Future Tense,* and *The Future Perfect Tense.* Verb tenses can be grouped according to the mood to which they belong (see *Moods*).

Careful – Do not assume that tenses with the same name in English and in French are used in the same way.

STUDY TIPS: TENSES

Pattern
- Start by comparing the new tense forms to the forms you already know for that verb, especially those that look or sound similar.
  - Identify the similarities with the other tenses to help you remember the new tense.
  - Identify the differences with the other tenses to help you avoid mixing them up.
- Remember that a verb that is irregular in one tense is not necessarily irregular in another.

Practice
1. To learn the forms of a simple tense, follow the instructions *Study Tips – Verb Conjugations.*
2. Apply the pattern you have just learned by writing and saying aloud another verb that follows the same pattern.
3. Rewrite the practice sentences of tenses you learned earlier using the new tense.

Flashcards
As you learn new tenses, separate the verb cards from your other cards and write down any irregular forms on the French side.

pouvoir	*to be able to / can*
Je peux	*I can*
Nous pouvons	*we can*
Ils peuvent	*they can (present)*
J'ai pu	*I was able to + infinitive (passé composé)*
pourr-	*(stem future/conditional)*

As you learn more verbs and tenses, you will be able to recognize more patterns and write less on the cards.

CHAPTER 17: THE PRESENT TENSE

> **ILLUSTRATIVE EXAMPLE**
>
> English: *Anna **reads** her favorite book while Max **plays** with his toys in the room; both **enjoy** their quiet afternoon.*
>
> French: Anna **lit** son livre préféré tandis que Max **joue** avec ses jouets dans la chambre; tous les deux **apprécient** leur après-midi tranquille.

The **Present Tense** shows that the action of the verb is happening now, in the present. This can mean: it's happening right now as the speaker talks, it happens regularly, it's a general truth.

> I *miss* you.
> She *works* too much.
> The moon *is* full every thirty days.

In English
There are three verb forms that indicate the present tense. Each form has a slightly different meaning:

Marc *works* from home.	Present
Marc *is working* from home.	Present Progressive
Marc *does work* from home.	Present Emphatic

Based on how a question is worded, you will automatically choose one of the three forms above for your answer.

> Where does Marc work? *He works* from home.
> Where is Marc now? *He is working* from home.
> Does Marc work from home? Yes, *he does work* from home.

In French
The present tense, called **le Présent**, is a **simple tense**. To form it, you add specific endings to the verb's stem (see *Verb Conjugation*).

In French, unlike in English, there's only one verb form for the present tense. This French present tense can express what English means with the *present, present*

60

progressive, and *present emphatic* tenses.

>Marc *works* from home.
>>works → **travaille**

>Marc *is working* from home.
>>is working → **travaille**

>Marc *does work* from home.
>>does work → **travaille**

Careful – In French, the present tense is shown by the verb ending itself, without needing auxiliary verbs like *is* or *does*. So don't translate these English auxiliary verbs; use the main verb in the present tense.

FRENCH FACT: HOMOPHONES
French has many homophones – words that sound the same but have different meanings. For example: **ver** *(worm)*, **vert** *(green)*, **vers** *(toward)*, and **verre** *(glass)*.

CHAPTER 18: PARTICIPLES

> **ILLUSTRATIVE EXAMPLE**
>
> English: *The **singing** birds woke me up this morning, and I noticed the **closed** windows kept out the noise last night.*
>
> French: *Les oiseaux **chantant** m'ont **réveillé** ce matin, et j'ai **remarqué** que les fenêtres **fermées** ont **bloqué** le bruit la nuit dernière.*

A **Participle** is a verb form used in two main ways: with an auxiliary verb to show specific tenses, or as an adjective to describe something.

>   She has *left* the company.
>   has: auxiliary + participle → past tense
>
>   All the doors and windows were *closed*.
>   closed: participle describing doors and windows → adjective

There are two types of participles: the **Present Participle** and the **Past Participle**.

Present Participle

In English
The present participle is easy to recognize because it is the **-ing** form of the verb: *working, studying, dancing, playing.*

The present participle is mainly used as the main verb in compound tenses with the auxiliary verb **to be** (see *Auxiliary Verbs*).

>   Joachim *is studying* really hard for his exam.
>   studying → present progressive of *to study*
>
>   She *was eating*.
>   was eating → past progressive of *to eat*

In French
The present participle, **le Participe Présent**, is formed by adding **-ant** ending to the stem of the **nous** form of the present tense:

mange~~ons~~ → mange**ant** *(eating)*
écout~~ons~~ → écout**ant** *(listening)*

Note that the present participle is used differently and less frequently in French than English.

Careful – Remember, French doesn't use participles like English does in constructions with auxiliary verbs + present participle (like *she is eating* or *they were arguing*). Instead, these constructions in English correspond to simple tenses in French.

*He **is eating***	Il **mange**
is eating → Present Progressive	mange → present
*They **were arguing***	Ils **se disputaient**
were arguing → Past Progressive	disputaient → imperfect
*She **will be coming** home soon*	Elle **rentrera** bientôt
will be coming → Future Progressive	rentrera → future

Past Participle

In English
The past participle is formed in several ways. It is the form of the verb that follows *I have*: *I have **spoken**, I have **written**, I have **worked**.*

The past participle has two primary uses:

    1. As the main verb in compound tenses with the auxiliary verb *to have*:

        *I have **said** all that was on my mind.*
        *She hasn't **seen** him in ten months.*

    2. As an adjective:

        Do you prefer to have a ***broken** window* or a ***fixed** window*?
        broken → describes the noun *window*
        fixed → describes the noun *window*

In French
The past participle, **le Participe Passé**, can be regular or irregular. Here are the endings for regular verbs:

- -er verbs → add -é to the stem
- -ir verbs → add -i to the stem
- -re verbs → add -u to the stem

INFINITIVE	STEM	PAST PARTICIPLE
manger	mang-	mang**é**
choisir	chois-	chois**i**
vendre	vend-	vend**u**

You will have to memorize the past participle of irregular verbs individually. As you can see in the examples below, they can be very different from the infinitive.

INFINITIVE	PAST PARTICIPLE
être	été
avoir	eu
prendre	pris
boire	bu
mettre	mis
savoir	su

Same as in English, the past participle can be used as the main verb of a compound tense or as an adjective.

1. **As the main verb in compound tenses** with the auxiliary verb **avoir** *(to have)* or **être** *(to be)*:

> Ils ont **mangé** le gâteau.
> *They have **eaten** the cake.*
>
> Marion est **allée** chercher sa sœur.
> *Marion has **gone** to pick up her sister.*

Many tenses are formed with the auxiliary verbs **avoir** or **être** + the past participle of the main verb. These tenses are discussed in various chapters of this handbook (see *The Past Tense, The Past Perfect Tense, The Future Perfect Tense,* and *The Conditional*).

2. **As an adjective that agrees with the noun** it modifies in gender and number (see *Descriptive Adjectives*):

la robe **achetée**
> la robe → noun, fem. sing. / achetée → adjective, fem. sing. (acheté + e)

*the **purchased** dress*

les plats **cuisinés**
> les plats → noun, masc. pl. / cuisinés → adjective, masc. pl. (cuisiné + s)

*the **cooked** dishes*

les assiettes **cassées**
> les assiettes → noun, fem. pl. / cassées → adjective, fem. pl. (cassé + es)

*the **broken** plates*

FRENCH FACT: EUPHONIC LIAISON

In French, sometimes the final consonant of one word links with the following word, creating what's called a **liaison** for smoother speech. For example, **les amis** *(the friends)* is pronounced *"lez-amis."*

Chapter 19: The Past Tense

> **ILLUSTRATIVE EXAMPLE**
>
> English: *After dinner, they **watched** a movie and then **went** for a walk. It **reminded** them about their childhood adventures.*
>
> French: *Après le dîner, ils ont **regardé** un film puis sont **allés** se promener. Ça leur **rappelait** leurs aventures d'enfance.*

The **Past Tense** is used to indicate that an action took place in the past.

   I *went* to the museum yesterday.

In English
There are several verb forms to indicate that the action took place in the past (a separate section is devoted to the past perfect, *I had traveled*).

I traveled	Simple Past
I have traveled	Present Perfect
I was traveling	Past Progressive
I used to travel	with helping verb *used to*
I did travel	Past Emphatic

The simple past is called "simple" because it uses just one word (like *traveled* in the example). Other past tenses are **compound tenses** because they use more than one word, like an auxiliary verb + a main verb (such as *was traveling* or *did travel*). See *Tenses*.

In French
There are two French tenses that correspond to all the English past verbal forms listed above: **le Passé Composé** and **l'Imparfait**. We will refer to these two tenses by their French names because they do not correspond to a specific English tense.

Le Passé Composé (Present Perfect)

The **Passé Composé** is formed with the auxiliary verb **avoir** *(to have)* or **être** *(to be)* conjugated in the present tense + the past participle of the main verb (see *Auxiliary*

Verbs and *Participles*).

J'ai acheté	I bought, I have bought, I did buy
Nous avons acheté	we bought, we have bought, we did buy

ai / avons → avoir
acheté → past participle of **acheter** *(to buy)*

Je **suis rentré**	I went home, I have gone home, I did go home
Ils **sont rentrés**	they went home, they have gone home, they did go home

suis / sont → être
rentré → past participle of **rentrer** *(to go home)*

Selection of the Auxiliary "Avoir" or "Être"

Most verbs use the auxiliary **avoir**. Therefore, it is easier for you to memorize the list of verbs conjugated with **être** and assume that the other verbs are conjugated with **avoir**.

There are about sixteen common verbs, sometimes called *verbs of motion*, that are conjugated with **être**. However, this term is not always accurate because some of these verbs, like **rester** *(to stay)*, don't involve motion. Also, some verbs that do involve motion, like **courir** *(to run)*, are conjugated with avoir. You can easily remember common *être verbs* by learning them in pairs of opposites:

aller	to go	venir	to come
retourner	to return	rester	to remain
entrer	to come in	sortir	to go out
arriver	to arrive	partir	to leave
monter	to climb / to go up	descendre	to go down
naître	to be born	mourir	to die
tomber	to fall		

Verbs derived from the above verbs are also conjugated with **être**: **rentrer** *(to return / to go home)*, **revenir** *(to come back)*, and **devenir** *(to become)*, among others. Note that all reflexive verbs are also conjugated with **être** (see *Reflexive Pronouns and Verbs*).

Agreement of the Past Participle

The rules of agreement of the past participle depend on whether the auxiliary verb is **avoir** or **être**.

Être – When the auxiliary verb is **être**, the past participle agrees in gender and number with the subject (see *Subjects*).

>Martin **est allé** au bureau.
>>Martin → subject, masc. sing.
>>allé → past participle, masc. sing.
>
>*Martin **went** to the office.*
>
>Manon **est allée** au magasin.
>>Manon → subject, fem. sing.
>>allée → past participle, fem. sing. (allé + e)
>
>*Manon **went** to the shop.*
>
>Martin et Manon **sont allés** à l'opéra.
>>Subjects: Martin → masc. sing. + Manon → fem. sing. = **ils**
>>allés → past participle, masc. pl. (allé + s)
>
>*Martin and Manon **went** to the opera.*

Avoir – When the auxiliary verb is **avoir**, the past participle agrees in gender and number of the direct object as long as the direct object comes before the verb (see the section on *Direct Objects* and *Direct Object Pronouns*).

- Direct object pronouns *always* come before the verb → past participle agrees with the antecedent of the pronoun.

>Joachim voulait le tout nouvel iPhone. Il **l'**a **acheté**.
>>iPhone → antecedent masc. sing.
>>l' → pronoun direct object masc. sing.
>>acheté → past participle, masc. sing.
>
>*Joachim wanted the newest iPhone. He **bought it**.*
>
>Joachim voulait les nouveaux AirPods. Il **les** a **achetés**.
>>AirPods → antecedent masc. pl.
>>les → pronoun direct object masc. pl.
>>achetés → past participle + s, masc. pl.
>
>*Joachim wanted the new AirPods. He **bought them**.*
>
>Joachim voulait ces assiettes. Il **les** a **achetées**.
>>assiettes → antecedent fem. pl.
>>les → pronoun direct object fem. pl.

achetées → past participle + es, fem. pl.
*Joachim wanted these plates. He **bought them**.*

- Direct object nouns can come *before* the verb → past participle agrees with the noun(s).

    Voici les **assiettes** que Joachim a **achetées**.
    assiettes → noun direct object fem. pl.
    achetées → past participle + es, fem. pl.
    *Here are the **plates** Joachim **bought**.*

    Les **produits** Apple qu'il a **achetés** sont neufs.
    les produits → direct objects masc. pl.
    achetés → past participle + s, masc. pl.
    *The Apple **products** he **bought** are new.*

- Direct object nouns can come *after* the verb → no agreement, the past participle remains in the masculine singular.

    Joachim a **acheté** ces **assiettes**.
    acheté → past participle masc. sing.
    assiettes → direct object after the verb, fem. pl.
    *Joachim **bought** these **plates**.*

Remember the following when using the **passé composé**:
- Determine whether the verb takes **avoir** or **être** as the auxiliary.
- Depending on which auxiliary verb is required, apply the appropriate rules of agreement.

L'Imparfait (Imperfect)

The **Imparfait** is a simple tense made from the stem of the 1st person plural of the present tense (regular and irregular verbs) + endings: **-ais, -ais, -ait, -ions, -iez, -aient**.

nous mange~~ons~~ → je mange**ais** *(I ate)*
nous regard~~ons~~ → elle regard**ait** *(she looked)*
nous cour~~ons~~ → ils cour**aient** *(they ran)*

Two English verb forms indicate that the **Imparfait** should be used in French:

1. The verb form includes, or could include: *used to, would*.

   *When I was young, I **used to** love candy.*
   *When I was young, I **would** love candy.*
   Quand j'étais jeune, j'**adorais** les bonbons.
       adorais → imparfait

2. The verb form is in the *past progressive* tense.

   *At this time yesterday, I **was working**.*
       was working → past progressive

   À cette heure hier, je **travaillais**.
       travaillais → imparfait

Apart from these two English verb forms, the English verb doesn't show whether you should use the **Imparfait** or the **Passé Composé**.

Selection: Le Passé Composé or l'Imparfait?

Whether to put a verb in the **Passé Composé** or the **Imparfait** often depends on the context. Here are a few guidelines.

- When the English verb can't include *used to, would* (see above), put the French verb in the **passé composé**.

   *What **did** you **do** last Thursday?*
   *I **went** out with some friends.*
       did do, went: cannot be replaced by *used to do, used to go*.
   Qu'**as**-tu **fait** jeudi dernier ?
   Je **suis sorti** avec des amis.
       as fait, suis sorti → passé composé

Compared to:
   *When we were young, what **did** you **cook** on Christmas Eve?*
   *I **cooked** roasted potatoes and turkey.*
       did cook, cooked: can be replaced by *used to cook, would cook*.
   Quand on **était** jeune, que **cuisinais**-tu au réveillon de Noël ?
   Je **cuisinais** des patates rôties et de la dinde.
       était, cuisinais → imparfait

- When more than one action was taking place at the same time in the past, to indicate what was going on → **Imparfait**; to indicate what happened →

Passé Composé.

*She **was sleeping** when they **knocked** on the door.*
> The actions was *sleeping* and *knocked* took place at the same time in the past: what was going on? She was sleeping → **imparfait**; what happened? They knocked. → **passé composé**.

Elle **dormait** quand ils **ont toqué** à la porte.
> dormait → imparfait
> ont toqué → passé composé

Compared to:
> *I **slept**, they **knocked** on the door, and we **had** breakfast together.*
>> The series of actions *slept, knocked* and *had* happened one after another in the past → **passé composé.**
>
> J'**ai dormi**, ils **ont toqué** à la porte et on **a pris** le petit déjeuner ensemble.
>> ai dormi, ont toqué, a pris → passé composé

Sometimes both tenses can fit, but usually one of the two is more logical.

Careful – English and French use a different tense in sentences with the word *since* or *for* (when *for* refers to a period of time).

- **In English** – The verb preceding *since* or *for* is in a past tense as the action began in the past and continues in the present.

    I haven't eaten meat since university.
    I haven't been eating meat since university.
    > have not been eating → past tense (still going on in the present)

    I haven't eaten meat for five years.
    I have not been eating meat for five years.
    > have not been eating → past tense (still going on in the present)

- **In French** - The verb preceding **depuis** *(since* or *for)* is in the present tense as the action began in the past and is continuing in the present.

    Je ne **mange** pas de viande **depuis** l'université.
    > mange → present
    > depuis → since

    *I **haven't eaten** meat since university.*
    *I **haven't been eating** meat since university.*

    Je ne **mange** pas de viande **depuis** cinq ans.
    > mange → present

71

depuis → for
*I **haven't eaten** meat **for** five years.*
*I **have not been** eating meat **for** five years.*

STUDY TIPS: LE PASSÉ COMPOSÉ

1. Auxiliary verb (avoir or être)

- Some students find it easier to remember the verbs that use **être** by pairing them with their opposites.
- You might also find it helpful to know that the first letters of the verbs that take **être** spell **Dr. Mrs. Vandertramp.**

Dr.	descendre, rester
Mrs.	monter, retourner, sortir
Vandertramp	venir, aller, naître, devenir, entrer, revenir, tomber, rentrer, arriver, mourir, partir

2. Main verb (past participle)

- Regular past participle: (see *Participles*)
- Irregular past participles: to be learned as vocabulary.

Practice

- Take out the verb cards that use **être** as the auxiliary verb. Look at the French side and write or say sentences in the **Passé Composé**. Do the same with the English side.
- Do the same with the verb cards that use **avoir** as the auxiliary verb.
- Once you are comfortable with verbs that use **être** and verbs that use **avoir**, mix the two piles together.
- Look at the English side and write or say French sentences in the **Passé Composé**. This time, remember both the auxiliary verb and the past participle.

Flashcards

Add to each of your verb flashcards the **je** of the **Passé Composé**. This will show you whether the verb is conjugated with **avoir** or **être** and will give you the past participle form of the main verb. For example:

comprendre	*to understand*
j'ai compris	*I understood*

Chapter 20: The Past Perfect Tense

> **ILLUSTRATIVE EXAMPLE**
>
> English: *She went to bed and fell asleep quickly exhausted from the day's activities, after she **had finished** her homework.*
>
> French: *Elle est allée au lit et s'est endormie rapidement, épuisée par les activités de la journée, après qu'elle **eut fini** ses devoirs.*

The **Past Perfect Tense**, also called **Pluperfect**, is used to express an action completed in the past before another action or event that also occurred in the past. You can compare this tense to the **Future Perfect**, which is used to indicate that one action precedes another in the future (see *The Future Perfect Tense*).

> He *realized* that he *had left* his phone.
> realized → simple past (1)
> had left → past perfect (2)
> > Both actions 1 and 2 occurred in the past, but action 2 preceded action 1. Therefore, action 2 is in the past perfect tense.

In English

The past perfect is formed with the auxiliary *had* + the past participle of the main verb: *I had slept, he had forgotten*. In conversation, *had* is often shortened to 'd.

Remember, verb tenses show when an action happens. If verbs in a sentence are in the same tense, it means the actions happened at the same time. To show that actions happened at different times, different tenses must be used.

Look at the following examples:

> The cat *was hiding* because the dog *was barking*.
> was hiding → past progressive (1)
> was barking → past progressive (2)
> Action 1 and action 2 took place at the same time.

> The cat *was hiding* because the dog *had barked*.
> was hiding → past progressive (1)
> had barked → past perfect (2)
> Action 2 took place before action 1.

In French

The past perfect, **le Plus-Que-Parfait**, is formed with the auxiliary verb **avoir** or **être** in the **Imparfait** + the past participle of the main verb: **j'avais dormi** *(I had slept)*, **il avait oublié** *(he had forgotten)*.

The rules of agreement of the past participle are the same as for the **Passé Composé**.

A verb is put in the **Plus-Que-Parfait** to indicate that the action of that verb happened before an action of the verb in the **Passé Composé** or the **Imparfait**.

Look at the order of events shown by the past tenses in the timeline below:

- Same verb tense → same moment in time
    *The cat **was hiding** because the dog **was barking**.*
    Le chat **se cachait** parce que le chien **aboyait**.
        se cachait, aboyait → imparfait (-1)
        Two actions in the **imparfait** (point -1) indicate that they took place at the same time in the past (before 0).

- Different verb tenses → different times
    *The cat **was hiding** because the dog **had barked**.*
    Le chat **se cachait** parce que le chien **avait aboyé**.
        se cachait → imparfait (-1)
        avait aboyé → plus-que-parfait (-2)
        The action in the **plus-que-parfait** (point -2) occurred before the action in the **imparfait** (point -1).

Careful – You can't always rely on spoken English to decide when to use the past perfect in French. Oftentimes, English permits the use of the simple past to describe an action that happened before another, as long as it's clear which action happened first.

> *Martin **forgot** (that) he **lost** his wallet.*
>   forgot, lost → simple past
> *Martin **forgot** (that) he **had lost** his wallet.*
>   forgot → simple past
>   had lost → past perfect

Although the two sentences above mean the same thing, only the sequence of tenses in the second sentence would be correct in French.

> Martin **a oublié** qu'il **avait perdu** son portefeuille.
>   a oublié → passé composé (-1)
>   avait perdu → plus-que-parfait (-2)
>   The action in the **plus-que-parfait** (point -2) indicates that it was completed before the other action (point -1).

FRENCH FACT: BORROWED WORDS
English has borrowed many words from French, like **rendezvous**, **cul-de-sac**, and **ballet**.

Chapter 21: The Future Tense

> **ILLUSTRATIVE EXAMPLE**
>
> English: We **are going to drive** to the beach tomorrow and we **will enjoy** the sunshine, **build** sandcastles and **swim** in the ocean all day long.
>
> French: Nous **allons conduire** à la plage demain et nous **profiterons** du soleil, **construirons** des châteaux de sable et **nagerons** dans l'océan toute la journée.

The **Future Tense** indicates that an action will take place sometime in the future.

> She*'ll attend* the event.

In English
The future tense is formed with the auxiliary *will* or *shall* + the dictionary form of the main verb. Note that *shall* is used in formal English (and British English), and *will* in everyday language. In conversation, *shall* and *will* are often shortened to *'ll*.

> Alexandre and Marion *will* go to town this afternoon.
> I*'ll* handle that matter tomorrow morning.

In French
There's no need for an auxiliary to show that an action will take place in the future. You indicate future time by using a simple tense formed with a stem, referred to as the **Future Stem** + endings: **-ai, -as, -a, -ons, -ez, -ont.**

- Future stem of regular verbs:

    -er verbs → infinitive
    -ir verbs → infinitive
    -re verbs → infinitive without final -e

INFINITIVE	FUTURE STEM	ENGLISH
manger	manger-	to eat
choisir	choisir-	to choose
prendre	prendr-	to take

Let's look at the conjugation of these verbs:

Je manger**ai**	Je choisir**ai**	Je prendr**ai**
Tu manger**as**	Tu choisir**as**	Tu prendr**as**
Il/Elle/On manger**a**	Il/Elle/On choisir**a**	Il/Elle/On prendr**a**
Nous manger**ons**	Nous choisir**ons**	Nous prendr**ons**
Vous manger**ez**	Vous choisir**ez**	Vous prendr**ez**
Ils/Elles manger**ont**	Ils/Elles choisir**ont**	Ils/Elles prendr**ont**

- The future stems of irregular verbs must be learned as vocabulary as they are unpredictable.

INFINITIVE	FUTURE STEM	ENGLISH
être	ser-	*to be*
avoir	aur-	*to have*
courir	cour-	*to run*
venir	viendr-	*to come*

Let's look at the conjugation of these verbs:

Je **serai**	J'**aurai**	Je **courrai**	Je **viendrai**
Tu **seras**	Tu **auras**	Tu **courras**	Tu **viendras**
Il/Elle/On **sera**	Il/Elle/On **aura**	Il/Elle/On **courra**	Il/Elle/On **viendra**
Nous **serons**	Nous **aurons**	Nous **courrons**	Nous **viendrons**
Vous **serez**	Vous **aurez**	Vous **courrez**	Vous **viendrez**
Ils/Elles **seront**	Ils/Elles **auront**	Ils/Elles **courront**	Ils/Elles **viendront**

Notice that whatever the stem, regular or irregular, the sound of the letter **r** is always heard before the future endings are added to the stem.

Careful – In English, we use the present tense after phrases like *as soon as*, *when*, and *by the time* for actions that will happen in the future. In French, you use the future tense instead.

> *As soon as I **know**, I **will inform** you.*
> know → present
> will inform → future

Dès que je **saurai**, je t'**informerai**.
> saurai → future
> informerai → future
> action to take place in the future ("as soon as I know...")

*He **will visit** when he **feels** better.*
> will visit → future
> feels → present

Il **rendra** visite quand il **se sentira** mieux.
> rendra visite → future
> se sentira → future
> action to take place in the future ("... when he will feel better")

French is stricter than English in its use of tenses.

The Immediate Future

In English and French, you can talk about an action that will happen in the near future without using the future tense. Instead, you can use a construction that suggests the future. This is called the **Immediate Future**.

In English
The immediate future is expressed with the verb *to go* in the present progressive tense + the infinitive of the main verb: *you are going to eat, they are going to see.*

similar meaning	
I am going to eat	**I will eat**
present progressive of *to go* + infinitive	future tense of *to eat*

In French
The same construction exists in French. It is called **le Futur Immédiat** or **le Futur Proche** because it refers to a future action that is considered closer in time than an action expressed by the future tense.

The immediate future is formed with the verb **aller** *(to go)* in the present tense + the infinitive of the main verb: **tu vas manger** *(you are going to eat)*, **ils vont voir** *(they are going to see)*.

Look at the difference between the forms of the immediate future and the future tense.

Je vais manger	**Je mangerai**
present of aller + infinitive (immediate future)	*future tense of manger (to eat)*

In spoken French, the immediate future often replaces the future tense.

STUDY TIPS: THE FUTURE TENSE

Pattern
1. Future stems (see above in this chapter)
2. Endings (see *Study Tips - Verb conjugations*)
   - The 1st, 2nd and 3rd persons singular, as well as the 3rd person plural, are identical to same persons in the present tense of the verb avoir: **-ai, -as, -a,** and **-ont**.
   - The 1st and 2nd person plural are identical to the same persons' endings of the present tense for most verbs: **-ons** and **-ez**.

Flashcards
On your verb cards, if a verb has an irregular future stem, add it too. Note: the future stem will also be the stem for the conditional (see *The Conditional*).

venir	to come
viendr-	*(stem: future/conditional)*

Practice
1. Separate the verbs with regular future stems.
   - Look at the French side. Write or say sentences using the verb in the future tense.
   - Look at the English side. Write or say the sentences in French using the verb in the future tense.
2. Separate the verbs with irregular future stems. Repeat the steps from 1 above.
3. Mix the pile of verbs with regular and irregular future stems. Repeat the steps from 1 above.

CHAPTER 22: THE FUTURE PERFECT TENSE

> **ILLUSTRATIVE EXAMPLE**
>
> <u>English:</u> *By the time we arrive, they **will have finished** setting up the decorations for the party, ensuring everything looks perfect for the guests.*
>
> <u>French:</u> *Quand nous arriverons, ils **auront fini** d'installer les décorations pour la fête, s'assurant que tout soit parfait pour les invités.*

The **Future Perfect Tense** is used to express an action that will occur before another action in the future or before a specific time in the future.

> By the time the film comes out, I *will have finished* the book.
> > film comes out → future event (2)
> > will have finished → future perfect (1)
> > Both actions 1 and 2 will occur at some future time, but action 1 will be completed before action 2 takes place. Therefore, action 1 is in the future perfect tense.
>
> We won't have the chance to meet; I *will have left* already.
> > to meet → future event (2)
> > will have left → future perfect (1)
> > Both actions 1 and 2 will occur at some future time, but action 1 will be completed before action 2 takes place. Therefore, action 1 is in the future perfect tense.

In English

The future perfect is formed with the auxiliary *will have* + the past participle of the main verb: *I will have left, you will have eaten*. In conversation, *will* is often shortened to *'ll*.

The future perfect is often used after expressions such as *by then, by that time, by + a date*.

> *By the time* the week is done, *she'll have finished* the project.
> *I'll have moved by* the end of the year.

In French

The future perfect, known as **le Futur Antérieur**, is formed with the auxiliary **avoir** or **être** in the future tense + the past participle of the main verb: **je serai parti** *(I will* *have left)*, **tu auras mangé** *(you'll have eaten)*.

The rules of agreement of the past participle are the same as for the **passé composé** (see *The Past Tense*).

As in English, a verb is put in the **futur antérieur** tense to indicate that the action of that verb will have taken place before the action of a verb in the future or before a specific future time.

Observe the sequence of the future tenses in the timeline below:

Verb Tense:	*Present*	*Future Perfect*	*Future*
	Présent	Futur Antérieur	Futur
	0	1	2
	---X--------------------------X-----------------------X---		

Time Action Takes Place: 0 → now
　　　　　　　　　　　　　　　1 → after 0 and before 2
　　　　　　　　　　　　　　　2 → after 1

*By the time **I move** to France, **I will have mastered** French.*
Quand je **déménagerai** en France, **j'aurai maîtrisé** le français.
　　déménagerai en France → futur (2)
　　j'aurai maîtrisé le français → futur antérieur (1)
　　The action in the futur antérieur (1) will occur before the action in the futur (2).

*Before you **wake up**, **I'll have gone**.*
Avant que tu **te réveilles, je serai parti**.
　　tu te réveilles → futur (2)
　　je serai parti → futur antérieur (1)
　　The action in the futur antérieur (1) will occur before the future event (2).

Careful – While English uses the present tense after conjunctions such as *when* (**quand**) and *as soon as* (**dès que**), French uses the futur antérieur.

*As soon as **she finishes** her dinner, **she'll go** straight to bed.*
　　finishes → present
　　will go → future

Quand elle **aura terminé** son dîner, elle **ira** directement au lit.
　　aura terminé → futur antérieur
　　ira → futur

> **FRENCH FACT: "R" SOUND**
>
> The French **r** sound can be notoriously difficult for non-native speakers to pronounce. It's often described as a guttural sound made at the back of the throat.

Chapter 23: Moods

> **ILLUSTRATIVE EXAMPLE**
>
> English: *She **believes** in you, so **do** your best, and I hope you **will succeed** in all your endeavors.*
>
> French: *Elle **croit** en toi, alors **fais** de ton mieux, et j'espère que tu **réussiras** dans toutes tes entreprises.*

Mood in grammar refers to the way verbs are used to express different purposes. For example, verb forms that state facts *(you are eating, you ate)* belong to one mood and the verb form that gives commands *(eat!)* belongs to another. Some moods have several tenses, while others have only one.

You should know the names of moods so that you understand them when you see these terms. As you learn verbs and their tenses, you will also learn when to use the different moods.

In English
Verbs can be in one of four moods:

1. The **Indicative Mood** is used to state facts or actions. This is the most common mood and most of the verbs you use in daily conversation are in the indicative mood. Most of the tenses you will learn in this handbook are in the indicative mood. For instance, *The Present Tense, The Past Tense,* and *The Future Tense.*

    Martin *learns* Spanish.
    → present indicative

    Julie *lived* here.
    → past indicative

    They *will leave* at the end of the week.
    → future indicative

2. The **Imperative Mood** is used to give commands or orders. This mood is not divided into tenses (see *The Imperative*).

    Martin, *do* your Spanish homework!
    Alice and Camille, *be* ready to leave in half an hour!

3. The **Subjunctive Mood** is used to express an attitude or feeling toward the action of the verb; it is subjective about it. In English, this mood is not divided into tenses (see *The Subjunctive*).

> The teacher requires that students *speak* a basic level of French.
> He wishes they *were* together.
> The boss asks that they *be* removed from the premises.

4. The **Conditional Mood** is primarily used to express:
   - A wish or desire more politely.
   - A hypothetical state of affairs or an event that can only be realized if another event occurs.

It has two tenses: the present conditional and the past conditional (see *The Conditional*).

> *Would you* drive me to the dentist?
> We *would* travel the world if we could afford it.
> Had he worked harder, he *would have* earned the promotion.

In French
Verbs can be in one of four moods:

1. As in English, the **Indicative Mood** is the most common and most of the tenses you will learn belong to this mood.
2. As in English, the **Imperative Mood** is used to give orders. It is not divided into tenses.
3. Unlike in English, the **Subjunctive Mood** is used very frequently. It has two main tenses: the *present subjunctive* and the *past subjunctive*. The term *present subjunctive* is used to distinguish it from the *present indicative* and the *present conditional* tenses.
4. As in English, the **Conditional Mood** has two tenses: the *present conditional* and the *past conditional*. The term *present conditional* is used to distinguish it from the *present indicative* and the *present subjunctive* tenses.

When there is no reference to mood, the tense belongs to the most common mood, which is the indicative.

FRENCH FACT: SUBJUNCTIVE MOOD
French has a tense called **le subjonctif**, used to express doubt, emotion, or uncertainty. It's notoriously tricky for learners.

CHAPTER 24: THE IMPERATIVE

> **ILLUSTRATIVE EXAMPLE**
>
> English: **Listen** carefully to the instructions and **complete** the assignment before you leave the classroom.
>
> French: **Écoute** attentivement les instructions et **termine** le devoir avant de quitter la salle de classe.

The **Imperative** is a verbal mood used to give someone an order. The **Affirmative Imperative** is an order to do something. The **Negative Imperative** is an order not to do something (see *Moods*).

> *Call me!*
> *Don't do that!*

In English

There are two types of commands, based on who is being told to do or not do something.

1. **"You" Command** – When an order is given to one or more persons, the dictionary form of the verb is used.

AFFIRMATIVE IMPERATIVE	NEGATIVE IMPERATIVE
Go to your room.	Don't go to your room.
Finish your plate.	Don't finish your plate.
Get in the car.	Don't get in the car.

2. **"We" Command** – When an order is given to oneself as well as to others, the phrase *let us* is used + the dictionary form of the verb. *Let us* is often contracted to *let's*, with the letter *u* replaced by an apostrophe.

AFFIRMATIVE IMPERATIVE	NEGATIVE IMPERATIVE
Let's go.	Let's not go.
Let's talk.	Let's not talk.

In French

Like in English, there are affirmative and negative commands. To form commands in French, most verbs use the present tense and drop the subject pronoun.

1. **"Tu" Command** – When an order is given to a person to whom one says *tu*, the *tu-form* of the present tense is used.

AFFIRMATIVE IMPERATIVE	NEGATIVE IMPERATIVE
Pars.	Ne pars pas.
Leave.	*Don't leave.*
Va dans ta chambre.	Ne vas pas dans ta chambre.
Go to your room.	*Don't go to your room.*

Note that in the imperative *-er* verbs drop the final *s* in the tu-form:

PRESENT TENSE	IMPERATIVE
Tu parles	Parle !
You speak	*Speak!*
Tu donnes	Donne !
You give	*Give!*

2. **"Vous" Command** – When an order is given to a person to whom one says *vous*, or if you address more than one person, the *vous-form* of the present tense is used.

AFFIRMATIVE IMPERATIVE	NEGATIVE IMPERATIVE
Partez.	Ne partez pas.
Leave.	*Don't leave.*
Allez dans vos chambres.	N'allez pas dans vos chambres.
Go to your rooms.	*Don't go to your rooms.*

3. **"Nous" Command** – When an order is given to oneself as well as to others, the *nous-form* of the present tense is used

AFFIRMATIVE IMPERATIVE	NEGATIVE IMPERATIVE
Partons.	Ne partons pas.
Let's leave.	*Let's not leave.*

Allons dans nos chambres.	N'allons pas dans nos chambres.
Let's go to our rooms.	*Let's not go to our rooms.*

In both English and French, if there is no subject pronoun in the sentence, it usually means it is an imperative (a command) and not a present tense sentence (see *The Present Tense*).

>Vous **venez** ce soir.
>*You **are coming** tonight.*
>→ present
>
>**Venez** ce soir.
>***Come** tonight.*
>→ imperative

Careful – French verbs in the affirmative imperative tense use a special set of object pronouns (see *Disjunctive Pronouns*).

FRENCH FACT: ÇA VA?
The phrase **Ça va ?** can mean *How are you?* or *Is it going?* depending on context. It's a very versatile expression that the French use on a daily basis.

Chapter 25: The Conditional

> **ILLUSTRATIVE EXAMPLE**
>
> <u>English:</u> *If I had seen you, I **would have said** hello, and if I have time tomorrow, I **would help** you with your project.*
>
> <u>French:</u> *Si je t'avais vu, je t'**aurais dit** bonjour, et si j'ai le temps demain, je t'**aiderais** avec ton projet.*

The **Conditional** is a verbal mood named because it is mainly used in sentences that express a condition (see *Moods*).

> *If I were wealthy, I would travel the world.*
>   were wealthy → condition
>   would travel → verb in the conditional

These hypothetical statements are made up of two clauses:
- The **If-Clause** – the clause starting with *if* states a condition → the verb is in the indicative mood, except for the verb *to be* that goes in the subjunctive mood.
- The **Result Clause** – the clause states what would occur if the condition were *fulfilled* → the verb is in the conditional mood.

The conditional mood has two tenses: a present and a past tense.

Present Conditional in If-Clauses

In English
The present conditional is formed with the auxiliary *would* + the dictionary form of the main verb: *I would come, she would talk, they would leave, I would go.*

> The present conditional is used in the following ways:
>
> 1. **In polite requests:**
>
>> *Would you please hand me my bag?*
>
> 2. **In the result clause of a hypothetical or contrary-to-fact statement.**
> When the condition refers to the present time, the result clause verb uses the present conditional, and the if-clause verb uses the simple past tense.

For the verb *to be*, use *were* in the subjunctive. This rule applies no matter which clause comes first.

> Joachim **would** travel the world if he **had** the means.
> would travel → present conditional
> had → simple past
> Hypothetical: Joachim does not have the means now; if he did, he would travel the world. There's a possibility of him having the means in the future and traveling the world.

> If Manon **were** in France, we **would meet** her in Paris.
> were → subjunctive
> would meet → present conditional
> Contrary-to-fact: Manon is not in France so we can't meet her.

In French

Unlike in English, you do not need an auxiliary to form the present conditional, **le Conditionnel Présent**. It is a simple tense formed with the future stem + the imperfect endings: **-ais, -ais, ait, -ions, -iez, -aient.** For example: je **viendrais** *(I would come)*, il **parlerait** *(he would speak)*, nous **mangerions** *(we would eat)*.

As in English, the present conditional is used in two ways:

1. In polite requests:

> **Pourriez-vous** me passer mon sac ?
> pourriez-vous → present conditional
> **Would you** please hand me my bag?

2. In the result clause of a hypothetical or contrary-to-fact statement.

When the condition refers to the present time, the result clause verb is in the present conditional and the **si** *(if)*-clause verb is in the **imparfait**, regardless which clause comes first in the sentence.

> Joachim **voyagerait** dans le monde s'il en **avait** les moyens.
> voyagerait → present conditional
> avait → imparfait
> Joachim **would** travel the world if he **had** the means.

Careful — The auxiliary *would* does not translate to the French conditional when it means *used to*, as in *she would talk while he painted*. In this case, *would talk* means *used to talk* and should be translated using the imperfect tense in French.

Also, note that in French, **si** contracts to **s'** before **il** for phonetic reasons. This contraction occurs to avoid the awkward pronunciation that would result from the sequence of the vowel sounds **si il**. That contraction does not apply to **si elle**, as the combination is easier to pronounce.

Past Conditional in If-Clauses

In English
The past conditional is formed with the auxiliaries *would have* + the past participle of the main verb: *I would have left, she would have drunk, we would have laughed.* In spoken English *would have* is often shortened to *would've*.

When the condition refers to the past, the result clause verb is in the past conditional and the if-clause verb is in the past perfect tense, regardless which clause comes first in the sentence.

> If Joachim **had had** the means, he **would have traveled** the world.
> had had → past perfect
> would have traveled → past conditional
> A fact: Joachim did not have the means, hence he did not travel the world.

In French
The past conditional, **le Conditionnel Passé**, is formed with the auxiliary **avoir** or **être** in the present conditional + the past participle of the main verb: je **serais parti**, elle **aurait bu**, nous **aurions ri** *(I would have left, she would have drunk, we would have laughed)*. The same rules of agreement apply as for the **passé composé** (see *The Past Tense*).

As in English, when the condition refers to time in the past, the result clause verb is in the past conditional and the **si** *(if)*-clause verb is in the **plus-que-parfait**, regardless which clause comes first in the sentence (see *The Past Perfect Tense*).

> Joachim **aurait voyagé** dans le monde, s'il **avait eu** les moyens.
> aurait voyagé → past conditional
> avait eu → plus-que-parfait
> Joachim **would have traveled** the world, if he **had had** the means.

> Si Joachim **avait eu** les moyens, il **aurait voyagé** dans le monde.
> avait eu → plus-que-parfait
> aurait voyagé → past conditional
> If Joachim **had had** the means, he **would have traveled** the world.

Summary: If-Clauses Sequence of Tenses

In English and in French the *if*-clause can come before or after the result clause, and the tense of one clause depends on the tense of the other.

- The condition is possible; if met, the result will take place now or in the future.

IF-CLAUSE ← → RESULT CLAUSE	
present	*future*
présent	futur

*If she **works** hard, she **will get** the promotion.*
    works → present
    will → future

Si elle **travaille** dur, elle ***aura*** la promotion.
    travaille → présent
    aura → futur

- The condition is unlikely; if met, the result will take place in the future.

IF-CLAUSE ← → RESULT CLAUSE	
simple past	*present conditional*
imparfait	conditionnel présent

*If she **worked** hard, she **would get** the promotion.*
    worked → simple past
    would get → present conditional

Si elle **travaillait** dur, elle **aurait** la promotion.
    travaillait → imparfait
    aurait → conditionnel présent

- The condition wasn't met in the past; but if it had been, the result would have occurred.

IF-CLAUSE ← → RESULT CLAUSE	
past perfect	*past conditional*
plus-que-parfait	conditionnel passé

*If she **had worked** hard, she **would have gotten** the promotion.*

had worked → past perfect
would have gotten → past conditional

Si elle **avait travaillé** dur, elle **aurait eu** la promotion.
    avait travaillé → plus-que-parfait
    aurait eu → conditionnel passé

Use of the Conditional in Indirect Speech

Direct Speech is when you quote exactly what someone said, word for word, using quotation marks. **Indirect Speech** is when you repeat or report what someone said without quoting them exactly.

In both English and French the conditional is used in the reported statement.

In English
Here is an example of a direct statement changed to an indirect statement.

DIRECT STATEMENT	Jean said: "Camille *will* leave tomorrow."
	said → past (1)
	will leave → future (2)
INDIRECT STATEMENT	Jean said that Camille *would* leave tomorrow.
	said → past (1)
	would leave → present conditional (2)

In the direct statement, action 2 is a quotation in the future tense. In the indirect statement, action 2 is called a **future-in-the-past** because it takes place after another action in the past, that first action being Jean said.

In French
As in English, the conditional is used in an indirect statement to express a future-in-the-past.

DIRECT STATEMENT	Jean a dit : « Camille **partira** demain. »
	a dit → passé composé (1)
	partira → futur (2)

INDIRECT STATEMENT	Jean a dit que Camille **partirait** demain.
	a dit → passé composé (1)
	partirait → conditionnel présent (2)

FRENCH FACT: ANIMAL SOUNDS

As in most other languages, in French, animals speak differently. For example: a rooster says **cocorico**, not *cock-a-doodle-doo*; cows say **meuh**, not *moo*; and cats say **miaou**, not *meow*.

Chapter 26: The Subjunctive

> **ILLUSTRATIVE EXAMPLE**
>
> <u>English:</u> *I want you to **be** happy and that you **have** everything you need to succeed.*
>
> <u>French:</u> *Je veux que tu **sois** heureux et que tu **aies** tout ce dont tu as besoin pour réussir.*

The **Subjunctive** is a verbal mood used to express a hypothesis, a wish, emotions, uncertainty, demands, or other similar attitude toward a fact or an idea (see *Moods*).

>I wish you *were* here with me.
>>I wish → subject's wish
>>were → subjunctive

>The boss asked that the employee *be* escorted off the premises.
>>asked → subject's demand
>>be → subjunctive

In English
The subjunctive verb forms are difficult to recognize because they are spelled like the dictionary form and the simple past tense.

INDICATIVE	SUBJUNCTIVE
She **works** a lot.	Her boss requires that she **work** a lot.
indicative present of to work	*subjunctive (same as dictionary form)*
I **am** home.	I wish I **were** home.
indicative present of to be	*subjunctive (same as past tense)*

The tense is rarely used and is mostly found in certain expressions or formal settings. In spoken English, it mostly comes after words like *require, demand,* and *wish*.

The Subjunctive is used in the following ways:

- **To express a hypothetical situation**
    >If she *were* more careful, she wouldn't make mistakes.
    >>were → past subjunctive

- **To express a wish or desire**

> I wish you *were* here.
> were → past subjunctive

- **To express commands, suggestions or demands**
  > The teacher demands that he *do* his homework.
  > do → present subjunctive

Note that you can't rely on English to know when to use the subjunctive in French and to determine how it is conjugated.

In French

Unlike in English, the subjunctive mood is used very frequently. There are various tenses, but the present and the past subjunctive are the most common ones, and we will cover them in this chapter.

The subjunctive mood is mainly used in **Dependent Clauses** (a group of words with a subject and a verb that cannot stand alone as a complete sentence) after certain verbs, expressions, and conjunctions when the subjects of the main and dependent clauses are different. Make sure to memorize these triggers (verbs, expressions, and conjunctions) for the subjunctive.

Here are a few examples. The dependent clause starting with **que** *(that)* is underlined.

- **Verbs of will or desire**
  Je **veux** que tu **viennes** à la fête.
  > veux → vouloir, subject je, indicative
  > viennes → venir, subject tu, subjunctive

  I **want** you to **come** to the party.
  (word-for-word: "I want that you come to the party")

  Elle **souhaite** que tu **sois** plus prudent.
  > souhaite → souhaiter, subject elle, indicative
  > sois → être, subject tu, subjunctive

  She **wishes** that you **be** more careful.
  (word-for-word: "She wants that you be more careful")

- **Expressions of necessity**
  Il **faut** que nous **trouvions** une solution.
  > faut → falloir, subject il, indicative
  > trouvions → trouver, subject nous, subjunctive

  It is **necessary** that we **find** a solution.

- **Verbs of doubt**
  Je ne **suis** pas certaine que tu **comprennes** le problème.

　　　　　suis → être, subject je, indicative
　　　　　comprennes → comprendre, subject tu, subjunctive
　　　*I **am** not certain that you **understand** the problem.*

- **Expressions of emotion**
  Il **est** furieux <u>que tu **aies** menti</u>.
  　　　est → être, subject il, indicative
  　　　aies → avoir, subject tu, subjunctive
  *He is furious <u>that you **lied**</u>.*

- **Expressions of opinion**
  Il **est** important <u>qu'elle **finisse** ses études</u>.
  　　　est → être, subject il, indicative
  　　　finisse → finir, subject elle, subjunctive
  *It **is** important <u>that she **finish** her studies</u>.*

Present Subjunctive

In English
The use of the present subjunctive is mostly noticeable with the verb *to be* where, for all subjects, *to be* changes to *be*. Let's look at the verb's conjugation:

I	be
You	be
He/She/It	be
We	be
You	be
They	be

Let's look at some examples:

　　　It is necessary that you *be* patient.
　　　　　be → present subjunctive

　　　It is important that we *do* our homework.
　　　　　do → present subjunctive

In French
The present subjunctive, also known as **le Subjonctif Présent**, is formed by taking the 3rd person plural (**ils/elles**) form of the verb in the present indicative, removing the -ent ending + adding the subjunctive endings: **-e, -es, -e, -ions, -iez, -ent.**

Let's look at the conjugation of the verb **parler** *(to speak)*:

Je	que je parle
Tu	que tu parle**s**
Il/Elle/On	qu'il/elle/on parle
Nous	que nous parl**ions**
Vous	que vous parl**iez**
Ils/Elles	qu'ils/elles parl**ent**

Remember that the subjunctive is mostly used in dependent clauses, which generally starts with **que** *(that)*.

> Il faut **que** tu **parles** à ton père.
> *It is necessary **that** you **speak** to your father.*
>
> Il est important **que** tu sois ici à l'heure.
> *It's important **that** you **be** here on time.*

Past Subjunctive

In English
The past subjunctive is distinguishable only with the verb *to be* where, for all subjects, *to be* changes to *were*. For other verbs, the past subjunctive form is identical to the simple past tense, making it indistinguishable from it in form. The context and the nature of the sentence determine its subjunctive use.

Let's look at the verb's conjugation:

I	were
You	were
He/She/It	were
We	were
You	were
They	were

Let's look at some examples:

> If she *were* here, she would help us.
>   were → past subjunctive

If he *did* his homework regularly, he would be getting better grades.
> *did* is used here in the sense of a hypothetical situation, which is a common context for the subjunctive mood in English.

In French

The past subjunctive, known in French as **le Subjonctif Passé**, is formed by taking the present subjunctive form of the auxiliary verb (**avoir** or **être**) + the past participle of the main verb.

Let's look at the conjugation of the verb **parler** *(to speak)* which uses **avoir** as auxiliary:

Je	que j'**aie parlé**
Tu	que tu **aies parlé**
Il/Elle/On	qu'il/elle/on **ait parlé**
Nous	que nous **ayons parlé**
Vous	que vous **ayez parlé**
Ils/Elles	qu'ils/elles **aient parlé**

Note that when a verb uses **avoir** as auxiliary, whether it's to form the past subjunctive or any compound tense in French, the past participle generally does not agree with the subject. For the rules of agreement of the past participle see the corresponding section in *The Past Tense*.

Let's now look at the conjugation of the verb **aller** *(to go)* which uses **être** as auxiliary:

Je	que je **sois allé(e)**
Tu	que tu **sois allé(e)**
Il/Elle/On	qu'il/elle/on **soit allé(e)**
Nous	que nous **soyons allé(e)s**
Vous	que vous **soyez allé(e)s**
Ils/Elles	qu'ils/elles **soient allé(e)s**

Note that when a verb uses **être** as the auxiliary verb, the past participle must agree in gender and number with the subject. That means:

- For **feminine subjects**, add an **e**:

Je suis contente que Marie **soit allée** à la fête.

       Marie → subj. fem. sing
       soit → auxiliary verb, 3rd pers. sing. subjunctive present of *être*
       allée → past participle with *e*
*I am happy that Marie **went** to the party.*

- For **plural subjects**, add an **s**:

Elle doute que les garçons **soient allés** à Paris.
       les garçons → subj. masc. pl.
       soient → auxiliary verb, 3rd pers. pl. subjunctive present of *être*
       allés → past participle with *s*
*She doubts that the boys **went** to Paris.*

- For **feminine plural subjects**, add **es**:

Il est possible que tes sœurs **soient allées** au marché.
       tes sœurs → subj. fem. pl.
       soient → auxiliary verb, 3rd pers. pl. subjunctive present of *être*
       allées → past participle with *es*
*It is possible that your sisters **went** to the market.*

STUDY TIPS: THE SUBJUNCTIVE

Pattern
when memorizing the forms of the present subjunctive, compare them to the forms of the present indicative. It will help you remember what makes them different.

Practice
Consistent practice is key to mastering the subjunctive. Try to write sentences using the subjunctive mood daily.

Flashcards
- Create a set of flashcards with verbs in the Present Subjunctive and another set with verbs in the Past Subjunctive.
- Use color coding to distinguish the verbs that take **avoir** and those that take **être** as auxiliary.
- Add an example sentence on each flashcard conjugating the verb in the subjunctive mood.

PRESENT SUBJUNCTIVE (SUBJONCTIF PRÉSENT)	
FRONT	**BACK**
Faire (il)	**Fasse**
To do	*do*
Il est important que...	Il est important qu'il **fasse** ses devoirs.
It's important that...	*It's important that he **do** his homework.*

PAST SUBJUNCTIVE (SUBJONCTIF PASSÉ)	
FRONT	**BACK**
Aller (vous, fem. plural)	**que vous soyez allées**
To go	*went*
Je suis contente que...	Je suis contente que vous soyez allées au musée.
I am happy that...	*I am happy that you went to the museum.*

- When reviewing flashcards, always try to use the verb in a full sentence. This helps reinforce not just the conjugation but also the correct context for using the subjunctive.
- Once the two sets of cards are done, combine them and shuffle your flashcards regularly to ensure you can recall the verb forms, auxiliary and usages in any order.

CHAPTER 27: ADJECTIVES

> **ILLUSTRATIVE EXAMPLE**
>
> English: *The **big** dog ran through the **green** field, chasing the **playful** cat under the **bright** sun.*
>
> French: *Le **grand** chien courait à travers le champ **vert**, poursuivant le chat **joueur**, sous le soleil **brillant**.*

An **Adjective** is a word that describes a noun or pronoun. There are different types of adjectives classified based on how they describe the noun or pronoun.

Descriptive Adjective – A descriptive adjective indicates a quality; it tells what kind of noun it is (see *Descriptive Adjectives*).

> Our cat has *big* ears.
> He has a very *friendly* wife.

Possessive Adjective – A possessive adjective indicates possession; it tells whose noun it is (see *Possessive Adjectives*).

> *Their* dog ran away.
> *Your* cousins are coming to visit.

Interrogative Adjective – An interrogative adjective asks a question about a noun (see *Interrogative Adjectives*).

> *Whose* bag is this?
> *What* did you order?

Demonstrative Adjective – A demonstrative adjective points out a noun (see *Demonstrative Adjectives*).

> *These* biscuits are delicious.
> *That* house is haunted.

In English
English adjectives usually do not change their form, regardless of the noun or pronoun described.

In French

The main difference between English and French adjectives is that English adjectives keep their form no matter what noun they're describing. But in French, adjectives change to agree with the gender and number of the noun they modify.

> **FRENCH FACT: PLURAL FORMS**
>
> While most nouns form their plural by adding an **s**, some don't follow this rule. For example: **cheval** *(horse)* becomes **chevaux** *(horses)*, **animal** becomes **animaux** *(animals)*, and **cheveu** *(hair)* becomes **cheveux** *(hairs)*.

CHAPTER 28: DESCRIPTIVE ADJECTIVES

> **ILLUSTRATIVE EXAMPLE**
>
> English: *The **big** elephant stood majestically under the **blue** sky, its **gray** skin shining in the **warm** sunlight.*
>
> French: Le **gros** éléphant se tenait majestueusement sous le ciel **bleu**, sa peau **grise** brillant sous le soleil **chaud**.

A **Descriptive Adjective** describes a noun or pronoun by indicating one or more of its qualities or characteristics.

>   This table is *heavy*.
>   table → noun described
>   heavy → descriptive adjective

In English
A descriptive adjective does not change form, regardless of the noun or pronoun it modifies.

>   The paintings are *beautiful*.
>   You have a very *beautiful* daughter.
>   The adjective *beautiful* is the same although the persons described are different in number (*paintings* is plural and *daughter* is singular).

In French
While English descriptive adjectives never change form, French descriptive adjectives do change form to agree in gender and number with the noun or pronoun they describe.

Most regular adjectives usually add an **-e** to the masculine form to make it feminine, and an **-s** to make it plural (feminine and masculine).

>   *The vase is **green**.*
>   Le vase est **vert**.
>   vase → masc. sing. → vert
>
>   *The grass is **green**.*
>   L'herbe est **verte**.
>   herbe → fem. sing. → vert + e

*The tools are **green**.*
Les outils sont **verts**.
  outils → masc. pl. → vert + s

*The plates are **green**.*
Les assiettes sont **vertes**.
  assiettes → fem. pl. → vert + es

When you learn a new adjective, make sure you learn how to make its feminine and plural forms.

Attributive and Predicate Adjectives

In English
Descriptive adjectives are divided into two groups based on how they connect to the noun they describe and modify.

1. A **Predicate Adjective** is connected to the noun it modifies, which is always the subject of the sentence, by a **linking verb** such as *to be, to feel, to look*.

The mouse is *cute*.
  mouse → noun described
  is → linking verb to be
  cute → predicate adjective

The garden looks *beautiful*.
  garden → noun described
  looks → linking verb to look
  beautiful → predicate adjective

2. An **Attributive Adjective** is connected directly to the noun it modifies and always precedes it.

The *cute mouse* ran away.
  cute → attributive adjective
  mouse → noun described

They are having lunch in the *beautiful garden*.
  beautiful → attributive adjective
  garden → noun described

In French

Like in English, descriptive adjectives in French can be either predicate or attributive adjectives. Predicate adjectives come after a linking verb like **être** *(to be)* and follow the same word order as in English.

But, while in English descriptive adjectives always come *before* the noun they describe, in French, most descriptive adjectives come *after* the noun, but not all.

> Ils ont visité un **site archéologique**.
> *They visited an **archeological site**.*

However, some common French descriptive adjectives come before the noun they modify.

> Boris est un **gentil chien** et Anémone est un **joli chat**.
> *Boris is a **good dog** and Anémone is a **beautiful cat**.*

Flashcards

1. Make flashcards with the adjective written twice on the French side: once with a masculine noun and once with a feminine noun. This will help you see the masculine and feminine forms of the adjective and whether it goes before or after the noun.

Un joli vase	A beautiful vase
Une jolie fleur	A beautiful flower

Un musée intéressant	An interesting museum
Une histoire intéressante	An interesting story

2. If the adjective has irregular singular or plural forms, indicate them.

Un nouveau savon	A new soap
Des nouveaux savons	Some new soaps
Le nouvel an	The new year
Les nouvelles années	The new years
Une nouvelle voiture	A new car

Practice

Write short sentences using the descriptive adjectives you learned, concentrating on the descriptive adjectives with irregular forms.

FRENCH FACT: FALSE FRIENDS

French has false friends and tricky words that look similar to English but have different meanings, such as **préservatif** *(condom)* and *preservative,* or **librairie** *(book shop)* and *library.*

CHAPTER 29: COMPARISON OF ADJECTIVES

> **ILLUSTRATIVE EXAMPLE**
>
> English: *The **taller** giraffe was **faster than** the **shorter** one, covering the savanna with **greater** agility and **more** grace.*
>
> French: *La girafe **plus grande** était **plus rapide que** la **plus petite**, parcourant la savane avec **plus** d'agilité et **plus** de grâce.*

A **Comparison of Adjectives** is used when two or more people (or things) have the same quality indicated by a descriptive adjective and you want to show which of them has more, less, or the same amount of that quality.

> Jeanne is *short* but Arnaud is *shorter.*
>   short → adjective that modifies Jeanne
>   shorter → adjective that modifies Arnaud

In English and in French there are two types of comparison: comparative and superlative.

Comparative

The comparison can indicate that one of the persons or things has more, less, or the same amount of that quality.

In English
Let's go over the three degrees of comparison:

   1. The comparison of **Greatest Degree** (more) changes form depending on the length of the adjective being compared.

- Short adjective + *-er* + **than**

    Arnaud is *shorter than* Jeanne.
    Tuesdays are *busier than* Mondays.

- *More* + longer adjective + ***than***

    Martin is *more* mature *than* his friend.
    This dress is *more* beautiful *than* the other one.

107

2. The comparison of **Lesser Degree** (less) is formed as follows: ***not as*** + adjective + ***as***, or ***less*** + adjective + ***than***.

> Jeanne is *not as* short *as* Arnaud.
> You are *less* mature *than* Martin.

3. The comparison of **Equal Degree** (same) is formed as follows: ***as*** + adjective + ***as***.

> The vegan cake is *as* tasty *as* the regular one.
> This dress is *as* beautiful *as* the other one.

In French

There are the same three degrees of comparison of adjectives as in English.

Like all French adjectives, French comparative adjectives agree with the noun they modify, in this case the subject of the sentence.

1. The comparison of **Greater Degree** is formed as follows: **plus** *(more)* + adjective + **que** *(than)*.

> Diane est **plus** travailleuse **que** Jérôme.
> > travailleuse: fem. sing. agrees with subject → Diane (fem. sing)
>
> *Diane is **more** hardworking **than** Jérôme.*

2. The comparison of **Lesser Degree** is formed as follows: **moins** *(less)* + adjective + **que** *(than)*.

> Jérôme est **moins** travailleur **que** Diane.
> > travailleur: masc. sing. agrees with subject → Jérôme (masc. sing)
>
> *Jérôme is **less** hardworking **than** Diane.*

3. The comparison of **Equal Degree** is formed as follows: **aussi** *(as)* + adjective + **que** *(as)*.

> Les desserts vegans sont **aussi** bons **que** les desserts normaux.
> > bons: masc. pl. agrees with subject → les desserts (masc. pl.)
>
> *The vegan desserts are as good as the regular desserts.*

Superlative

The superlative is used to indicate the highest and lowest degrees of a quality.

In English
Let's go over the two degrees of the superlative:

1. The superlative of **Greatest Degree** is formed differently depending on the length of the adjective.

- *The* + short adjective + *-est*
  Blue whales are *the largest* animals.
  Fridays are *the busiest.*

- *The most* + long adjective
  This dress is *the most beautiful.*
  Their plan is *the most complicated.*

2. The superlative of **Lowest Degree** is formed as follows: **the least** + adjective.

This dress is *the least beautiful.*
Their plan is *the least complicated.*

In French
As in English, there are two degrees of the superlative:

1. The superlative of **Greatest Degree** is formed as follows: **le, la,** or **les** (depending on the gender and number of the noun described) + **plus** *(most)* + adjective.

Marion est **la plus grande** de la famille.
  la plus grande → fem. sing.
*Marion is **the tallest** in the family.*

Ce chien est **le plus beau** de la bande.
  le plus beau → masc. sing.
*This dog is **the most beautiful** of the bunch.*

Martin et Clémence sont **les plus patients** de la classe.
  les plus patients → masc. pl.
*Martin and Clémence are **the most patient** in the class.*

2. The superlative of **Lowest Degree** is formed as follows: **le, la,** or **les** (depending on the gender and number of the noun described) + **moins** *(less)* + adjective.

Marion est **la moins loquace** du groupe.
*Marion is **the least talkative** of the group.*

Careful – In English and in French, a few adjectives have irregular forms of comparison that you will have to memorize.

ADJECTIVE	Cette marque est mauvaise.
	This brand is bad.

COMPARATIVE	Cette marque est pire.
	This brand is worse.

SUPERLATIVE	Cette marque est la pire.
	This brand is the worst.

The English comparative form *better* can be used as a comparative adjective or a comparative adverb. In French, it has different forms for each use and follows the rules for adjectives or adverbs (see *Adverb or Adjective?*).

Better comparing nouns = comparative of the adjective *good* (**bon**) → **meilleur** (adjective agrees with the noun it modifies):

*The film is **good** but the book is **better**.*
Le film est **bon** mais le livre est **meilleur**.

Better comparing verbs = comparative of the adverb *well* (**bien**) → **mieux** (adverb does not change form):

*We eat **well** here but **better** there.*
On mange **bien** ici mais **mieux** là-bas.

FRENCH FACT: INTERNATIONAL INFLUENCE
French has a strong influence on diplomatic and cultural affairs worldwide, being one of the official languages of international organizations like the United Nations.

CHAPTER 30: POSSESSIVE ADJECTIVES

> **ILLUSTRATIVE EXAMPLE**
>
> English: **My** cat loves to sleep in **his** cozy bed, while **her** dog prefers to play with **its** favorite toy.
>
> French: **Mon** chat aime dormir dans **son** lit douillet, tandis que **son** chien préfère jouer avec **son** jouet préféré.

A **Possessive Adjective** is a word that indicates who possesses the noun.

> Whose phone is this? It's *my* phone.
> possessor → me
> phone → object possessed

In English

Like subject pronouns, possessive adjectives are identified according to the person they represent.

SINGULAR POSSESSOR		
1st PERSON		my
2nd PERSON		your
3rd PERSON	Masculine	his
	Feminine	her
	Neutral	its

PLURAL POSSESSOR	
1st PERSON	our
2nd PERSON	your
3rd PERSON	their

A possessive adjective changes according to the possessor, regardless of the noun possessed.

> Is it Camille's phone? Yes, it is *her* phone.
> Is it Joachim's phone? Yes, it is *his* phone.
>> Although the object possessed is the same *(phone)*, different possessive adjectives *(her and his)* are used because the possessors are different *(Camille and Joachim)*.

Is it Camille's wallet? Yes, it is *her* wallet.
Are these Camille's earrings? Yes, they are *her* earrings.
> Although the objects possessed are different *(phone and earrings)*, the same possessive adjective *(her)* is used because the possessor is the same *(Camille)*.

In French

Like in English, French possessive adjectives change depending on who the possessor is. But unlike English, they also change to agree with the gender and number of the noun they describe.

Let's look at French possessive adjectives to see how they are formed. We have divided them into two groups.

Singular Possessor

1st, 2nd, and 3rd pers. sing.: *my, your* (tu-form), *his, her, its.*

In French, each possessive adjective has three forms based on the gender and number of the noun: masculine singular, feminine singular, and plural (same for both genders).

To choose the correct possessive adjective:

1. Indicate the possessor with the first letter of the possessive adjective.

my	m
your	t- (tu form)
his her its	s

2. Choose the ending according to the gender and number of the noun possessed.

- Noun possessed is masculine singular or feminine singular beginning with a vowel → add **-on**

Martin mange **mon** sandwich.	Martin eats **my** sandwich.
Martin mange **ton** sandwich.	Martin eats **your** sandwich.
Martin mange **son** sandwich.	Martin eats **his/her** sandwich.

mon, ton, son → masc. sing.
sandwich → noun possessed, masc. sing.

Justine est **mon** amie.	*Justine is **my** friend.*
Justine est **ton** amie.	*Justine is **your** friend.*
Justine est **son** amie.	*Justine is **his/her** friend.*

mon, ton, son → masc. sing. because noun starts with a vowel
amie/friend → noun possessed

- Noun possessed is feminine singular beginning with a consonant → add **-a**

Voici **ma** cuisine.	*Here's **my** kitchen.*
Voici **ta** cuisine.	*Here's **your** kitchen.*
Voici **sa** cuisine.	*Here's **his/her** kitchen.*

ma, ta, sa → fem. sing.
cuisine/kitchen → noun possessed

- Noun possessed is plural → add **-es**

J'ai apporté **mes** habits.	*I brought **my** clothes.*
J'ai apporté **tes** affaires.	*I brought **your** things.*
J'ai apporté **ses** habits.	*I brought **his/her** clothes.*

mes, tes, ses → masc. pl.
affaires/things → fem. pl.
habits/clothes → masc. pl.

3. Select the proper form according to the two steps above.

Let's apply the above steps to examples:

*Marie is looking for **her** sister.*
   1. Possessor: her → 3rd pers. sing. → **s-**
   2. Noun possessed: **sœur** *(sister)* → feminine singular → **a**
   3. Selection: **s- + -a**

Marie cherche **sa** sœur.

*Marie is looking for **her** brother.*
   1. Possessor: her → 3rd pers. sing. → **s-**
   2. Noun possessed: **frère** *(brother)* → masculine singular → **on**

113

3. Selection: s- + -on
Marie cherche **son** frère.

Careful – Ensure the ending of the possessive adjective agrees with the noun it describes, not the person who owns it. Context usually shows if you mean *his* or *her*.

Plural Possessor

1st, 2nd, and 3rd pers. pl.: *our, your* (vous-form), *their*.

In French, each of these possessive adjectives has two forms depending on whether the noun possessed is singular or plural.

- Noun possessed is singular → **notre, votre,** or **leur**:

Hercule est **notre** chien.	*Hercule is **our** dog.*
N'oubliez pas **votre** sac !	*Don't forget **your** bag!*
Ils vont chercher **leur** lessive.	*They are going to pick up **their** laundry.*

- Noun possessed is plural → **nos, vos,** or **leurs**:

Camille range **nos** affaires.	*Camille is putting away **our** things.*
Laissez-moi prendre **vos** manteaux.	*Let me take **your** coats.*
As-tu acheté **leurs** billets ?	*Did you buy **their** tickets?*

Although **votre** and **vos** are usually used for the second person plural, they can refer to one person when used in a formal address (see *Subject Pronouns*).

Careful – Make sure that you use the same *you* form, either familiar or formal, for both the verb and the possessive adjective: "You are late to your meeting" would be either: *Tu es en retard pour ta réunion* or *Vous êtes en retard pour votre réunion*.

Summary

Here is a chart you can use as a reference.

POSSESSOR SINGULAR		NOUN POSSESSED	
		SINGULAR	PLURAL
my	masc. | fem. + vowel | fem.	mon, mon, ma	mes
your (**tu** form) | **vous** (formal form)	masc. | fem. + vowel | fem.	ton, ton, ta	tes
		votre	vos
his, her, its	masc. | fem. + vowel | fem.	son, son, sa	ses

POSSESSOR PLURAL	NOUN POSSESSED	
	SINGULAR	PLURAL
our	notre	nos
your	votre	vos
their	leur	leurs

Note: In English and in French, possession can also be indicated with the possessive form: *Mary's dress, the teacher's book* → la robe de Marie, le livre du professeur (see *The Possessive*).

STUDY TIPS: POSSESSIVE ADJECTIVES

Pattern
It will be easy for you to establish a pattern if you follow our instructions under **Singular Possessor** and **Plural Possessor** above in this chapter.
 	
Practice
1. Sort out your noun flashcards and select a few of the following:
    • all masculine nouns
    • feminine nouns beginning with a consonant
    • feminine nouns beginning with a vowel
 	
2. Look at the French side of the cards and say the noun with the correct form of the possessive adjective. Focus on the singular forms *mon, ton,* and *son* because they are the forms that change.
 	
| **le jardin** | *garden* |
| mon jardin, ton jardin, etc. | |
| **la maison** | *house* |
| ma maison, ta maison, etc. | |
| **l'adresse (fem.)** | *address* |
| mon adresse, ton adresse, etc. | |

3. Look at the English side and go through the cards saying the French equivalent of the noun with the correct form of the possessive adjective, again concentrating on the singular forms.

Flashcards

1. For practice, make cards for each person (1st, 2nd, and 3rd singular and plural) with examples showing the different forms. Include an example with a feminine singular noun that starts with a vowel.

Mon manteau, ma veste, mes outils, mon école (fem.)	*my (coat, jacket, tools, school)*
Ton manteau, ta veste, tes outils	*your*
Votre (manteau, veste), vos (manteaux, vestes, outils)	*your*

2. On the card for the 3rd person singular, to reinforce the fact that *his*, *her* and *its* can be either *son* or *sa*, write French sentences with 3rd pers. sing. possessive adjectives modifying masculine and feminine singular nouns.

Il mange son sandwich	*He eats his/her sandwich.*
Elle mange son sandwich.	*She eats her/his sandwich.*
Il porte sa chemise.	*He wears his/her shirt.*
Elle porte sa chemise.	*She wears her/his shirt*

Chapter 31: Interrogative Adjectives

> **ILLUSTRATIVE EXAMPLE**
>
> English: **Which** car do you prefer, the red one or the blue one? **What** movie are we watching tonight? **Whose** phone is ringing?
>
> French: **Quelle** voiture préférez-vous, la rouge ou la bleue ? **Quel** film regardons-nous ce soir ? **À qui** est ce téléphone qui sonne ?

An **Interrogative Adjective** is a word that asks for information about a noun.

What flavors of ice cream would you like?
→ asks information about the noun *flavors*

In English

The words *which* and *what* are called interrogative adjectives when they modify a noun and are used to ask for more information about that noun.

Which dessert do you prefer?
What book are you reading?

In French

There is only one interrogative adjective: **quel**. As all French adjectives, it changes to agree in gender and number with the noun it modifies. So, you must always start by analyzing the noun to choose the correct form.

- Noun modified is masculine singular → **quel**
    ***Which** dish are you ordering?*
        plat *(dish)* → masculine singular
        which → masculine singular → quel
    Quel plat commandes-tu ?

- Noun modified is masculine plural → **quels**
    ***Which** dishes are you ordering?*
        plats *(dishes)* → masculine plural
        which → masculine plural → quels
    Quels plats commandes-tu ?

- Noun modified is feminine singular → **quelle**
    ***What** is your favorite flower?*

117

fleur *(flower)* → feminine singular
what → feminine singular → quelle
Quelle est ta fleur préférée ?

- Noun modified is feminine plural → **quelles**
What are your favorite flowers?
fleurs *(flowers)* → feminine plural
which → feminine plural → quelles
Quelles sont tes fleurs préférées ?

When the noun and the interrogative adjective are next to one another, it is easy to identify the noun modified. However, the noun modified is harder to identify when it is separated from the interrogative adjective. As you can see in the examples below, changing the sentence structure will help you find the noun that the interrogative adjective must agree with.

Which is your least favorite color?
Restructure: *"Which color is your least favorite?"*
Quelle est la couleur que tu préfères le moins ?
couleur → fem. sing.

What is your favorite dessert?
Restructure: *"What dessert is your favorite?"*
Quel est ton dessert préféré ?
dessert → masc. sing.

Careful – The word *what* isn't always an interrogative adjective. In the sentence *What is for dinner?* it's an interrogative pronoun (see *Interrogative Pronouns*). It's important to know the difference because in French, different words are used for each, and they follow different rules.

FRENCH FACT: ORIGINS OF FRENCH
The French language has evolved significantly due to its historical influences, including from Latin, Germanic languages, and Arabic.

CHAPTER 32: DEMONSTRATIVE ADJECTIVES

> **ILLUSTRATIVE EXAMPLE**
>
> English: **This** book is interesting, but **that** one is boring. **These** cookies are delicious, but **those** are too sweet.
>
> French: **Ce** livre est intéressant, mais **ce** livre-**là** est ennuyeux. **Ces** cookies sont délicieux, mais **ceux-là** sont trop sucrés.

A **Demonstrative Adjective** is a word used to point out a noun or to point to a noun.

> *This* meal is delicious.
> → points out the noun meal

In English
The demonstrative adjectives are *this* and *that* in the singular and *these* and *those* in the plural. They are rare examples of English adjectives changing based on whether the noun they modify is singular or plural: *this* changes to *these* and *that* changes to *those* when they modify a plural noun.

SINGULAR	PLURAL
this house	*these* houses
this woman	*these* women

This and *these* refer to persons or objects near the speaker, and *that* and *those* refer to persons or objects away from the speaker.

In French
There is only one demonstrative adjective: **ce**. As all French adjectives, it agrees in gender and number with the noun it modifies. So, always start by analyzing the noun in order to choose the correct form.

- Noun modified is masculine singular and starts with a consonant → **ce**
    Ce chat est sale.
        chat *(cat)* → masculine singular
        this → masculine singular → ce
    This/that cat is dirty.

119

- Noun modified is masculine singular and starts with a vowel → **cet**
    Cet écran de télévision est énorme.
        écran *(screen)* → masculine singular, starts with a vowel
        this → masculine singular before a vowel → cet
    This/that TV screen is enormous.

- Noun modified is feminine singular → **cette**
    Cette carotte est moisie.
        carotte *(carrot)* → feminine singular
        this → feminine singular → cette
    This/that carrot is rotten.

- Noun modified is plural → **ces**
    Ces légumes doivent être rangés.
        légumes *(vegetables)* → plural
        these → plural → ces
    These/those vegetables need to be put away.

To distinguish between what is close to the speaker from what is far from the speaker, **-ci** *(here)* or **-là** *(there)* can be added after the noun.

   Ces fruits-**ci** sont frais; **ces** fruits-**là** sont vieux.
   These *fruits (here) are fresh;* ***those*** *fruits (there) are old.*

Notice the accent on **là** to distinguish it from the definite article **la** *(the)* which doesn't have an accent.

FRENCH FACT: NASAL SOUNDS
French has unique nasal vowel sounds represented by combinations of letters such as **on, en,** and **un**, which are challenging to pronounce for non native French speakers. These nasal sounds are frequently found under different forms but sound similar: **-ant, -im, -ent, -ont, -ain**, etc.

Chapter 33: Adverbs

> **ILLUSTRATIVE EXAMPLE**
>
> English: *She **quickly** ran downstairs to catch the bus **early**. He **carefully** and **quietly** examined the painting in the museum.*
>
> French: Elle est descendue **rapidement** les escaliers pour attraper le bus **tôt**. Il a examiné la peinture **soigneusement** et **silencieusement** dans le musée.

An **Adverb** is a word that describes a verb, an adjective, or another adverb. It indicates manner, degree, time, or place.

    Manon speaks different languages *well*.
        speaks → verb
        well → adverb

    The dog is *very* hairy.
        very → adverb
        hairy → adjective

    Marcus spoke *too soon*.
        too → adverb
        soon → adverb

In English

There are different types of adverbs:

- An **Adverb of Manner** answers the question *how?* Adverbs of manner are the most common and are easy to recognize because they end with **-ly.**

    Jean folds the sheets *neatly*.
        Neatly describes the verb *folds*; it indicates how Jean folds the sheets.

- An **Adverb of Degree** answers the question *how much?*

    She is *quite* happy with her results.

- An **Adverb of Time** answers the question *when?*

    They are leaving *later* in the day.

- An **Adverb of Place** answers the question where?

> There are mosquitoes *everywhere*.

In French

Most adverbs of manner can be recognized by the ending **-ment** that corresponds to the English ending **-ly.**

rapide**ment**	*quickly*
prudem**ment**	*carefully*
facile**ment**	*easily*

Adverbs must be memorized as vocabulary items. Just like prepositions and conjunctions, adverbs are invariable; meaning they never change form.

Careful – While in English adverbs tend to be placed after the subject of the sentence, in French they are usually placed after the verb.

> I **never** forget my phone and wallet.
> I → subject

> Je n'oublie **jamais** mon téléphone et portefeuille.
> oublie → verb

Adverb or Adjective?

Since adverbs are invariable and French adjectives must agree with the noun they modify, it is important to tell them apart. If a word describes (modifies) a noun, it's an adjective. If it describes a verb, an adjective, or another adverb, it's an adverb.

> Your husband is a *great* cook.
> > *Great* modifies the noun *cook*; it is an adjective.

> Your husband cooks *well*.
> > *Well* modifies the verb *cooks*; it is an adverb.

When you write a sentence in French, always make sure that adjectives agree with the noun or pronoun they modify and that adverbs remain unchanged.

> The **old** man reads the newspaper **peacefully**.
> > *Old* modifies the noun *man*; it is an adjective. *Peacefully* modifies the verb *reads* (it describes how the man read); it is an adverb.

Le **vieil** homme lit le journal **paisiblement**.
> vieil homme → masc. sing.
> paisiblement → adverb

*The **blond** woman walked **rapidly**.*
> *Blond* modifies the noun *woman*; it is an adjective. *Rapidly* modifies the verb *walked* (it describes how the woman walked); it is an adverb.

La femme **blonde** marchait **rapidement**.
> femme blonde → fem. sing.
> rapidement → adverb

*The **new** employees work **diligently**.*
> *New* modifies the noun *employees* → adjective
> *Diligently* modifies the verb *work* → adverb

Les **nouveaux** employés travaillent **diligemment**.
> nouveaux → adjective masc. pl.
> diligemment → adverb

Careful – In English, we often use adjectives instead of adverbs when speaking. However, in French, using an adjective as an adverb is incorrect; you must use an adverb instead.

*She walks real slow. → She walks **really slowly**.*
> really → adverb that modifies the verb walks
> slowly → adverb that modifies the adverb really

Elle marche **vraiment rapidement**.
> vraiment → adverb
> rapidement → adverb

STUDY TIPS: ADVERBS	
Flashcards	
1. Create flashcards for each French adverb you learn and its English equivalent.	

rarement	*rarely*

2. When you learn the placement of adverbs in a sentence, add sample sentences illustrating their placement.

Il ne parle jamais d'elle.	*He never speaks about her.*
Il n'a jamais parlé d'elle.	*He never spoke about her.*

Chapter 34: Conjunctions

> **ILLUSTRATIVE EXAMPLE**
>
> English: *She wants to go to the beach **but** he prefers to stay home. **Although** it's raining, they decided to have a picnic.*
>
> French: *Elle veut aller à la plage **mais** il préfère rester à la maison. **Bien qu'**il pleuve, ils ont décidé de faire un pique-nique.*

A **Conjunction** is a word that links two or more words or groups of words.

> There are two options: left *and* right.
> and → conjunction

> She went home *because* she wasn't feeling well.
> because → conjunction

In English
There are two kinds of conjunctions: coordinating and subordinating.

- A **Coordinating Conjunction** joins words, **phrases** (groups of words without a verb), or **clauses** (groups of words with a verb). The main coordinating conjunctions are *and, but, or, nor, for,* and *yet.*

    > left *or* right
    >   left → word
    >   right → word
    >   or → conjunction

    > at the end of the hall *and* on the left
    >   at the end of the hall → phrase
    >   on the left → phrase
    >   and → conjunction

    > I was invited *but* I didn't want to go.
    >   I was invited → clause
    >   I didn't want to go → clause
    >   but → conjunction

In the last example, both *I was invited* and *I didn't want to go* are complete thoughts on their own. Each one is called a **Main Clause** because it's a full sentence by itself.

The coordinating conjunction *but* links these two main clauses together.

- A **Subordinating Conjunction** connects a main clause to a dependent clause. The dependent clause doesn't express a complete thought on its own, so it needs the main clause to make sense. There are various types of dependent clauses. When a subordinating conjunction introduces a clause, it's called a **Subordinate Clause**. Common subordinating conjunctions include words like *before, after, since, although, because, if, unless, so that, while, that,* and *when.*

    The subordinate clauses in the sentences below are underlined. As you can see, they are not complete sentences and each is introduced by a subordinating conjunction.

    Although I wasn't feeling well, I still went.
    although → subordinating conjunction

    You came *because* you wanted to see me.
    because → subordinating conjunction

    She won't get promoted *unless* she works hard.
    unless → subordinating conjunction

In French

Conjunctions must be memorized as vocabulary items. Just like adverbs and prepositions, conjunctions are invariable, meaning they never change form. Make sure you memorize the conjunctions that are followed by the subjunctive mood instead of the indicative (see *The Subjunctive*).

STUDY TIPS: CONJUNCTIONS AND THE SUBJUNCTIVE

Flashcards

1. Create flashcards for each French conjunction and their English equivalent.

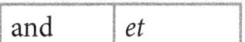

| and | *et* |

2. When you learn the subjunctive, indicate whether the French conjunction is followed by a verb in the indicative or the subjunctive mood. Add an example to help.

parce que (+ ind.)	*because*
Elle est rentrée parce qu'elle est fatiguée.	*She went home because she is tired.*
bien que (+ subj.)	*although*
Elle n'est pas rentrée bien qu'elle soit fatiguée.	*She didn't go home although she was tired.*

Practice

Write a series of sentences using the different conjunctions. Make sure to put the following verb in the subjunctive, if the conjunction requires it.

CHAPTER 35: PREPOSITIONS

> **ILLUSTRATIVE EXAMPLE**
>
> English: The book is **on** the table **next to** the lamp, and the cat is **under** the chair **between** the cushions.
>
> French: Le livre est **sur** la table **à côté de** la lampe, et le chat est **sous** la chaise **entre** les coussins.

A **Preposition** is a word that connects nouns to other words in a sentence, often showing a relationship in time or space. It can link nouns to nouns, nouns to verbs, or different parts of a sentence to each other.

> I have an appointment *with* my doctor.
>   with → preposition
>   my doctor → object of preposition
>   with my doctor → prepositional phrase

The noun or pronoun following the preposition is called the **Object of the Preposition**. The preposition + its object is called a **Prepositional Phrase**.

In English

Prepositions normally indicate location, direction, or time.

- **Prepositions showing location or direction:**

  > Marion is walking *toward* the bus stop.
  > The cat sleeps *in* the closet.
  > Maxime's book is *on* the table.
  > Your phone is *beside* the computer.

- **Prepositions showing time and date:**

  > The meeting is *at* 3:00 pm.
  > We're having a party *on* Saturday.
  > Julie's birthday is *in* November.
  > Anaïs will be away *for* two weeks.
  > They have been in a relationship *since* high school.

In French

You will have to memorize prepositions as vocabulary, paying special attention to their meaning and how to use them in French. Just like adverbs and conjunctions, prepositions are invariable: they never change form.

Careful – Prepositions can be tricky. Every language uses prepositions differently. Don't assume that the same preposition used in English will work in French, or vice versa. Sometimes, you might not need a preposition in one language when you need it in the other. Look at the following examples:

ENGLISH	FRENCH
CHANGE OF PREPOSITION	
to depend **on**	dépendre **de**
to be interested **in**	s'intéresser **à**

PREPOSITION	NO PREPOSITION
to listen **to**	écouter
to pay **for**	payer

NO PREPOSITION	PREPOSITION
to enter	entrer **dans**
to need	avoir besoin **de**

A dictionary will usually tell you which preposition to use with a verb. Don't try to translate an English verb + preposition directly into French word-for-word (see *Consulting the Dictionary* in the chapter titled *The Infinitive*).

STUDY TIPS: PREPOSITIONS

Flashcards

When making flashcards for prepositions, remember that one English preposition can have several French equivalents and vice versa. Always learn a preposition in a short sentence to see how it is used.

1. Prepositions indicating the position of one object or person in relation to another are the easiest to learn because the English preposition usually has only one French equivalent.

sur	on (top of)
Le chat est sur le toit.	*The cat is on the roof.*
derrière	*behind*
Margaux marche derrière Carl.	*Margaux walks behind Carl.*

2. Prepositions like *to, at, in* (for places) and *by, on, in* (for transportation) have many French equivalents because they change based on the noun that follows. Instead of making separate cards for these prepositions, add them on the correct noun cards.

l'opéra	*opera*
Nous allons à l'opéra.	*We are going to the opera.*
la gare	*train station*
Il va à la gare.	*He's going to the train station.*
le ferry	*ferry*
Ils y vont en ferry.	*They are going there by ferry.*
à pied	*on foot*
Je vais au musée à pied.	*I am going to the museum on foot.*

3. When you learn a verb that is usually followed by a preposition + noun, indicate the preposition on the verb card and write a short sentence to show how to use it.

entrer (dans)	*to enter*
J'entre dans votre chambre.	*I am entering your room.*

4. When you learn a verb that requires a preposition when it is followed by an infinitive, indicate the preposition on the verb card and write a short sentence to show how to use it.

essayer de + infinitive	*to try*
Je vais essayer d'être plus productif.	*I will try to be more productive.*

Practice
1. Using the examples from point 1 above, think of two objects (or people) and write French sentences using prepositions to show the positions of the objects (or people) relative to each other.
2. Using the examples from point 2 above, sort out the noun cards that indicate a place or a means of transportation. Create short sentences using these nouns with the correct prepositions.

Chapter 36: Objects

> **ILLUSTRATIVE EXAMPLE**
>
> <u>English:</u> *She handed **him** a **book**, which he promptly placed on the **shelf**. Meanwhile, the cat pursued the **mouse** under the table.*
>
> <u>French:</u> Elle **lui** a remis un **livre**, qu'il a rapidement placé sur **l'étagère**. Pendant ce temps, le chat a poursuivi la **souris** sous la table.

An **Object** is a noun or pronoun that indicates who or what the action of the verb is aimed at.

> Julien reads a *book*.
> reads → verb
> book → object

> We helped the *stranger*.
> helped → verb
> stranger → object

> You bought a *car*.
> bought → verb
> car → object

Verbs can be classified as to whether or not they require a direct object to complete its meaning (see below).

- A **Transitive Verb** (*v.t.* in the dictionary) is a verb that requires a direct object to complete its meaning *(to give, to say)*.

    > Margaux *gave* the gift.
    > gave → transitive

- An **Intransitive Verb** (*v.i.* in the dictionary) is a verb that doesn't require a direct object to complete its meaning *(to rain, to fall)*.

    > They *laughed*.
    > laughed → intransitive

- Verbs that can be **both transitive and intransitive** are verbs that can take a direct object (transitive) or not take a direct object (intransitive). Such verbs include *to eat, to begin, to finish, to read, to sing,* etc.

She *eats* an apple.
>the verb *eats* has a direct object *an apple* → transitive

She *eats*.
>the verb *eats* has no direct object → intransitive

Now let's look at the three types of objects: *direct objects, indirect objects,* and *objects of a preposition*. Because noun and pronoun objects are identified in the same way, we will only use noun objects in the examples here (see *Nouns*). For examples with pronoun objects, see *Direct Object Pronouns, Indirect Object Pronouns,* and *Disjunctive Pronouns*.

Direct Object

In English
A direct object is a noun or pronoun that directly receives the action of the verb, without a preposition in between. It answers the question *whom?* or *what?* after the verb.

>Julien reads a book.
>>Julien reads *what?* A book.
>>A book is the direct object.

In French
As in English, a direct object is a noun or pronoun that directly receives the action of the verb, without a preposition.

>*Maxime listens to **Camille**.*
>Maxime écoute **Camille**.
>>No preposition separates **Camille** from the verb **écoute** *(listens to)*.
>>Therefore, Camille is a direct object.

>*They played **the game**.*
>Ils ont joué **le jeu**.
>>No preposition separates **le jeu** *(the game)* from the verb **joué** *(played)*.
>>Therefore, le jeu is a direct object.

As with English verbs, French verbs can be transitive or intransitive depending on whether or not they are followed by an object.

Indirect Object

In English
An indirect object is a noun or pronoun that receives the action of the verb indirectly. It usually comes with a preposition and answers the question *to whom?* or *to what?* after the verb.

> George gave a gift to *his sister.*
>> He gave a gift *to whom?* His sister.
>> His sister is the indirect object.

> I sent flowers to *my grandmother.*
>> I sent flowers to *whom?* My grandmother
>> My grandmother is the indirect object.

In French
As in English, an indirect object is a noun or pronoun that receives the action of the verb indirectly, with the preposition **à** *(to)* relating it to the verb.

> George a donné un cadeau **à sa sœur.**
> *George gave a gift* **to his sister.**

> J'ai envoyé des fleurs **à ma grand-mère.**
> I sent flowers **to my grandmother.**

Nouns that are indirect objects are easy to spot in French because they always come after the preposition **à**. Remember to look for the accent to tell it apart from **a** without an accent, which means *has* (the 3rd person singular present of the verb **avoir**).

Sentences with a Direct and Indirect Object

A sentence can have both a direct object and an indirect object, which can be nouns or pronouns. Here, we will focus on sentences with nouns as direct and indirect objects.

In English
When a sentence has both a direct and an indirect object, the following two orders of words are possible:

1. Subject (S) + verb (V) + indirect object (IO) + direct object (DO):

Jonathan gave Marion a book.
  Who gave a book? Jonathan.
  Jonathan is the subject.
  Jonathan gave *what*? A book.
  A book is the direct object.
  Jonathan handed a book *to whom*? Marion.
  Marion is the indirect object.

2. Subject (S) + verb (V) + direct object (DO) + to + indirect object (IO):

Jonathan gave a book to Marion.
  Jonathan → S
  gave → V
  a book → DO
  Marion → IO

The first structure, under point 1, is the most common. However, because there is no *to* preceding the indirect object, it is more difficult to identify its function than in the structure under point 2.

No matter the word order, the words in the two sentences above have the same function because they answer the same questions: *to what?* and *to whom?* Always ask questions to find the function of words in a sentence.

In French

Unlike in English, when a sentence has both a direct and an indirect object there is only one word order possible (point 2): subject (S) + verb (V) + direct object (DO) + à (to) + indirect object (IO).

  Jonathan a donné **un livre à Marion.**
    Jonathan → S
    a donné → V
    un livre → DO
    Marion → IO
  Jonathan gave a **book to Marion.**
  Jonathan gave **Marion a book.**

Object of a Preposition

In English

An object of a preposition is a noun or pronoun that comes after a preposition (other than *to*) and shows who or what receives the action of the verb. (Objects of the preposition *to* are considered indirect objects and are discussed above.) It answers the question *whom?* or *what?* asked after the preposition.

> Jean bought flowers *for his wife.*
> > Jean bought flowers for *whom?* His wife.
> > *His wife* is the object of the preposition *for.*
>
> I paid for lunch with *my credit card.*
> > I paid for lunch with *what?* My credit card.
> > *My credit card* is the object of the preposition *with.*

In French

As in English, an object of a preposition is a noun or pronoun that receives the action of the verb through a preposition other than **à** *(to).*

> Jean a acheté des fleurs **pour sa femme.**
> *Jean bought flowers **for his wife.***
>
> J'ai payé le déjeuner **avec ma carte de crédit.**
> *I paid for lunch with **my credit card.***

Relationship of a Verb to Its Object

The relationship between a verb and its object is often different in English and in French. For example, a verb might have a direct object in English but an indirect object in French, or an object of a preposition in English but a direct object in French. So, when you learn a French verb, it's important to know if it needs a preposition and which one.

Here are differences you are likely to encounter:

1. ENGLISH: object of a preposition → FRENCH: direct object

> *I am waiting for **my taxi.***
> > I am waiting for *what?* My taxi.
> > *My taxi* is the object of the preposition *for*
>
> J'attends **mon taxi.**
> > *to wait for* → **attendre**
> > Function in French: direct object

Many common verbs require an indirect object or an object of a preposition in English, but a direct object in French, for example:

to ask for	*demander*
to search for	*chercher*
to pay for	*payer*

2. ENGLISH: direct object → FRENCH: indirect object

*He answers **emails** during his work day.*
    He answers *what?* Emails.
    Emails is the direct object.

Il répond à **des emails** durant sa journée de travail.
    to answer → **répondre à**
    Function in French: indirect object

A few common verbs require a direct object in English and an indirect object in French. Check these examples:

to please	*plaire à*
to resist	*résister à*
to forgive	*pardonner à*

3. ENGLISH: direct object → FRENCH: object of a preposition

*I am entering the **museum**.*
    I am entering *what?* The museum.
    The museum is the direct object.

J'entre dans **le musée.**
    to enter → **entrer dans**
    Function in French: object of the preposition **dans**

It's really important to be able to tell apart the three types of objects. Let's look at pronouns as an example. In French, when you're talking about the English pronoun *him*, the word you use depends on whether *him* is receiving the action directly (**le**) or indirectly (**lui**).

Summary

You can figure out the different types of objects in a sentence by seeing if they answer a question with a preposition, and if they do, figuring out which preposition it is.

- **Direct Object** – An object that receives the action of the verb directly, without a preposition.
- **Indirect Object** – An object that receives the action of the verb indirectly, through the preposition *to*.
- **Object of a Preposition** – An object that receives the action of the verb through a preposition other than *to*.

Careful – Always figure out what function a word plays in the language you're using. Don't try to apply English rules to French.

FRENCH FACT: CIRCUMFLEX ACCENT

The circumflex accent ^ often denotes a missing letter in French. For example: **hôpital** *(hospital)* used to be hospital, and **forêt** used to be *forest*.

CHAPTER 37: DIRECT OBJECT PRONOUNS

> **ILLUSTRATIVE EXAMPLE**
>
> English: *During the movie, she passed **me** the popcorn, and I shared **it** with everyone around **me**.*
>
> French: *Pendant le film, elle **m'**a passé le popcorn, et je **l'**ai partagé avec tout le monde autour de moi.*

A **Direct Object Pronoun** is a word that replaces a noun and functions as a direct object of a verb (see *Pronouns* and *Objects*).

> Julie works with *him*.
> > Julie works with *whom?* Answer: him.
> > *Him* is the direct object of the verb works with.

In this chapter we will look at direct object pronouns. Other object pronouns are studied in *Indirect Object Pronouns* and *Disjunctive Pronouns*.

In English
Most object pronouns are different from subject pronouns. The same form is used for direct object pronouns, indirect object pronouns, and disjunctive pronouns.

	SUBJECT PRONOUN	OBJECT PRONOUN
SINGULAR		
1st PERSON	I	me
2nd PERSON	you	you
3rd PERSON	he, she, it	him, her, it
PLURAL		
1st PERSON	we	us
2nd PERSON	you	you
3rd PERSON	they	them

Let's look at two examples of direct object pronouns.

> She loves *him*.
> > she → subject pronoun
> > him → direct object pronoun

We found *them*.
> we → subject pronoun
> them → direct object pronoun

In French

Just like in English, pronouns used as the direct object in a sentence are different from those used as the subject. But in French, direct and indirect objects have different forms.

Now, let's check out French direct object pronouns and see how they are formed. We've split them into two groups.

- **1st and 2nd person sing. and pl. (me, you, us)**

    The direct object pronouns of the 1st and 2nd persons have only one form per person. Just select the form you need from the chart below.

	SUBJECT	DIRECT OBJECT	SUBJECT	DIRECT OBJECT
SINGULAR				
1st PERSON	*je*	*me*	*I*	*me*
2nd PERSON	*tu*	*te*	*you*	*you*
PLURAL				
1st PERSON	*nous*	*nous*	*we*	*us*
2nd PERSON	*vous*	*vous*	*you*	*you*

To simplify our examples, we have used the verb *to watch* (**regarder**) because both the English and the French verbs take a direct object.

> *Arnaud watches **me**.*
> 1. Identify the verb: to watch
> 2. What is the French equivalent: **regarder**
> 3. Does the French verb need a preposition before an object: no
> 4. Function of pronoun in French: direct object
> 5. Selection: **me**
>
> Arnaud **me** regarde.
>
> *Arnaud watches **you**.*
> Arnaud **te** regarde.
> Arnaud **vous** regarde.

*Arnaud watches **us**.*
Arnaud **nous** regarde.

Understanding when to use **nous** and **vous** can be tricky. Not only are they both used for the subject and the object, but they're also both placed before the verb. But here's a tip: check the verb. Remember, verbs agree with their subject. If **nous** is the subject, the verb will end in **-ons**. If it doesn't, then **nous** is probably the object. The same goes for **vous**. If it's the subject, regular verbs will end in **-ez.**

Nous nous regardons.
We watch each other.

Vous nous regardez.
You watch us.

- **3rd person sing. and pl. (him, her, it, them)**
  The direct object pronouns for the 3rd person singular have different forms depending on whether the thing they're replacing is masculine or feminine. So, it agrees with the gender of the word it replaces.

  There is only one form for them.

	SUBJECT	DIRECT OBJECT	SUBJECT	DIRECT OBJECT
SINGULAR				
MASCULINE	il	le	*he, it*	*him, it*
FEMININE	elle	la	*she, it*	*her, it*
PLURAL				
MASCULINE	ils	les	*they*	*them*
FEMININE	elles			

For our examples we have again used the verb *to watch* (**regarder**) because both the English and French verbs take a direct object.

*Is he watching Anatole? Yes, he is watching **him**.*
Regarde-t-il Anatole ? Oui, il **le** regarde.

*Do you watch Marine? Yes, I watch **her**.*
Regardes-tu Marine ? Oui, je **la** regarde.

*Can you watch the boys? Yes, I can watch **them**.*

Peux-tu regarder les garçons ? Oui, je peux **les** regarder.

It as a direct object requires that you establish the gender of the noun it replaces (meaning, its antecedent).

Are you watching the film? Yes, I am watching it.
    Antecedent: *film* → **film** → masculine
    Gender of it: masculine → **le**
Regardes-tu le film ? Oui, je **le** regarde.

Did you watch the ad? Yes, I watched it.
    Antecedent: *ad* → **publicité** → feminine
    Gender of it: feminine → **l'** (la + verb *avoir* starting with a vowel)
As-tu regardé la publicité ? Oui, je **l'**ai regardée.

Unlike English where direct object pronouns are placed after the verb, in French they are usually placed before the verb.

Careful – Make sure you establish the correct type of object for the French verb, which might not always be the same as the object used with the English verb (see *Relationship of a Verb to Its Object* within the *Objects* chapter). For object pronouns used with verbs in the affirmative imperative, see *Disjunctive Pronouns*.

FRENCH FACT: FRENCH ACADEMY

The **Académie Française** is an institution founded in 1635 with the mission of preserving the French language. They publish dictionaries, regulate grammar and usage, and even invent French equivalents for new foreign words.

Chapter 38: Indirect Object Pronouns

> **ILLUSTRATIVE EXAMPLE**
>
> English: *She sent **us** a postcard from her vacation, telling **us** about her adventures in the mountains.*
>
> French: Elle **nous** a envoyé une carte postale de ses vacances, **nous** racontant ses aventures dans les montagnes.

An **Indirect Object Pronoun** is a word that replaces a noun and functions as an indirect object of a verb (see *Pronouns and Objects*).

> *Marie-Jeanne sent **me** a message.*
> Marie-Jeanne sent a message to *whom?* Answer: *me*.
> *Me* is the indirect object of the verb *sent*.

In this chapter we will look at indirect object pronouns. Other object pronouns are studied in *Direct Object Pronouns* and *Disjunctive Pronouns*.

In English

Most object pronouns are different from subject pronouns. The same form is used for direct object pronouns, indirect object pronouns, and disjunctive pronouns.

	SUBJECT PRONOUN	OBJECT PRONOUN
SINGULAR		
1st PERSON	I	me
2nd PERSON	you	you
3rd PERSON	he, she, it	him, her, it
PLURAL		
1st PERSON	we	us
2nd PERSON	you	you
3rd PERSON	they	them

Let's look at two examples of indirect object pronouns.

She sent a package to **him**.
    she → subject pronoun
    him → indirect object pronoun

They explained the rules to **us**.
    they → subject pronoun
    us → indirect object pronoun

In French

Just like in English, pronouns used as indirect objects are different from those used as subjects. But in French, direct and indirect object pronouns don't always have the same form.

Unlike nouns that are indirect objects, indirect object pronouns don't have the preposition **à** *(to)* before them. Now, let's look at how French indirect object pronouns are formed. We've split them into two groups.

- **1st and 2nd persons sing. and pl. (me, you, us)**
  The indirect object pronouns of the 1st and 2nd persons are the same as the direct object pronouns. Just select the form you need from the chart below.

	SUBJECT	INDIRECT OBJECT	SUBJECT	INDIRECT OBJECT
SINGULAR				
1st PERSON	je	me	*I*	*(to) me*
2nd PERSON	tu	te	*you*	*(to) you*
PLURAL				
1st PERSON	nous	nous	*we*	*(to) us*
2nd PERSON	vous	vous	*you*	*(to) you*

To simplify our examples, we have used the verb *to show to* (**montrer à**) because both the English and French verbs take an indirect object.

*Jeanne shows her house to **me**.*
    1. Identify the verb: to show
    2. What is the French equivalent: **montrer**
    3. Is the French verb followed by **à**: yes
    4. Function of the pronoun in French: indirect object
    5. Selection: **me**
*Jeanne **me** montre sa maison.*

*Jeanne shows her house to **you**.*
Jeanne **te** montre sa maison.
Jeanne **vous** montre sa maison.

*Jeane shows her house to **us**.*
Jeanne **nous** montre sa maison.

Figuring out the function of **nous** and **vous** can be tricky. Not only are they both used for the subject and the object, but they're also both placed before the verb. But here's a tip: check the verb. Remember, verbs agree with their subjects. If **nous** is the subject, the verb will end in **-ons**. If it doesn't, then **nous** is probably the object. The same goes for **vous**. If it's the subject, regular verbs will end in **-ez.**

Nous vous montrons la maison.
*We are showing the house to **you**.*

Vous nous montrez la maison.
*You are showing the house to **us**.*

- **3rd person sing. and pl. (him, her, it, them)**
  The indirect object pronouns of the 3rd persons have different forms depending on whether they refer to a person, a thing or an idea.

  1. **Person** – a singular and a plural form:

	SUBJECT	INDIRECT OBJECT	SUBJECT	INDIRECT OBJECT
SINGULAR				
MASCULINE	il	lui	he, it	him, it
FEMININE	elle		she, it	her, it
PLURAL				
MASCULINE	ils	leur	they	them
FEMININE	elles			

*Is Maxence talking to your brother? No, he's not talking **to him**.*
1. Identify the verb: to talk
2. What is the French equivalent: **parler**
3. Is the French verb followed by **à**: yes
4. Function of the pronoun in French: indirect object
5. Number of antecedent: singular (brother)
6. Selection: **lui**

Est-ce que Maxence parle à ton frère ? Non, il ne **lui** parle pas.

*Is Maxence talking to your parents? No, he's not talking **to them**.*
    1 - 4. See above.
    5. Number of antecedent: plural (parents)
    6. Selection: **leur**

Est-ce que Maxence parle à tes parents ? Non, il ne **leur** parle pas.

The 3rd person indirect object pronoun is the same for both males and females. To know if it refers to a male or female, you have to look at the context and what has been said before.

2. Thing and idea – one form → **y**

*Did you reply to the email? Yes, I replied to **it**.*
1. Identify the verb: to reply
2. What is the French equivalent: **répondre**
3. Is the French verb followed by **à**: yes
4. Function of the pronoun in French: indirect object
5. Type of antecedent: thing (the email)
6. Selection: **y**

Avez-vous répondu à l'email ? Oui, j'**y** ai répondu.

In French, indirect object pronouns are usually placed before the verb, unlike English where they are placed after the verb.

Careful – Make sure you establish the correct type of object for the French verb, which might not always be the same as the object used with the English verb (see *Relationship of a Verb to Its Object* within the *Objects* chapter). For object pronouns used with verbs in the affirmative imperative see *Disjunctive Pronouns*.

Questions to Ask Yourself When Choosing French Direct and Indirect Object Pronouns

DO → Direct object of the French verb
IO → Indirect object of the French verb

ME - 1st pers. sing		
Is it a DO?		Is it an IO?
→ **me** ←		

YOU - 2nd pers. sing. & pl.		
Familiar or singular? Is it a DO? Is it an IO? **te**		Formal or plural? **vous**

HIM - 3rd pers. sing.		
Is it a DO? **le**		Is it an IO? **lui**

HER - 3rd pers. sing.		
Is it a DO? **la**		Is it an IO? **lui**

IT - 3rd pers. sing.		
Is it a DO?		Is it an IO?
What is the gender of the antecedent?		
Masculine	Feminine	
le	**la**	**y**

US - 1st pers. pl.
nous

THEM - 3rd pers. pl.		
Is it a DO?	Is it an IO?	
	Is the antecedent a person or a thing?	
les	If a person	If a thing
	leur	**y**

Pattern

Learn the forms of direct and indirect object pronouns separately.

1. Look for similarities between direct object pronouns and other parts of speech. What similarities can you think of?
    - 1st & 2nd pers. sing.: initial **m-** and **t-** same as the first letters of the possessive adjectives (**mon, ton**)
    - 1st & 2nd pers. pl.: same as subject pronouns
    - 3rd pers. sing. & pl.: same as definite articles

2. When you learn indirect object pronouns, look for similarities with direct object pronouns and other parts of speech. What similarities do you notice?
- 1st, 2nd pers. sing. & pl.: same forms for direct and indirect object pronouns
- 3rd pers. pl.: indirect object pronoun is the same as the singular form of the 3rd pers. pl. possessive adjective **leur**. Careful: the possessive adjective has a singular and plural form (**leur, leurs**), while the indirect object pronoun has only one form, **leur**.

Practice

1. Since function determines a pronoun's form, it is important to learn object pronouns in a sentence.

2. Write a series of short French sentences with masculine, feminine and plural direct and indirect objects. Then rewrite the sentences replacing the object with the correct object pronoun.

Il mange le gâteau	He eats the cake
Il **le** mange	He eats **it**
Elle répond à Jean	She replies to Jean
Elle **lui** répond	She replies to **him**

Flashcards

1. On the subject pronoun flashcards, add sentences illustrating the pronoun's direct and indirect object forms.

elle	she, it
je **la/le** regarde	I watch **her/him/it**
je **lui** envoie un email	I send **him/her** an email

2. Practice by going through the cards on the English side and creating French sentences illustrating the various object pronoun forms.

FRENCH FACT: GLOBAL REACH
French is the only language, besides English, that is taught in every country in the world.

CHAPTER 39: DISJUNCTIVE PRONOUNS

> **ILLUSTRATIVE EXAMPLE**
>
> English: *I went to the park with **them**, while you went to the mall with **him** to buy groceries.*
>
> French: Je suis allé au parc avec **eux**, tandis que **toi**, tu es allé au centre commercial avec **lui** pour faire des courses.

A **Disjunctive Pronoun**, also called a **Stressed** or **Tonic Pronoun**, is mainly used to give a one-word answer to a question or as the object of a preposition (see *Pronouns* and *Objects*).

> Who's responsible for this mess? *Her*.
> My parents went to the restaurant without *me*.

In this chapter we will look at disjunctive pronouns. Other types of pronouns are studied in *Direct Object Pronouns* and *Indirect Object Pronouns*.

In English
Most object pronouns are different from subject pronouns. The same form is used for direct object pronouns, indirect object pronouns, and disjunctive pronouns.

	SUBJECT PRONOUN	DISJUNCTIVE PRONOUN
SINGULAR		
1st PERSON	I	me
2nd PERSON	you	you
3rd PERSON	he, she, it	him, her, it
PLURAL		
1st PERSON	we	us
2nd PERSON	you	you
3rd PERSON	they	them

Disjunctive pronouns are used primarily in two situations:

    1. **In short answers** when the identity of the person we refer to is obvious from the context:

Who are you talking about? *Her.*
Who will be staying with us? *Me.*

2. When the **pronoun is an object of a preposition:**

I am going to the party *with you.*
  with → preposition

They will wait *for* me.
  for → preposition

In French
Most disjunctive pronouns, known as **les Pronoms Personnels Toniques**, have a different form than direct and indirect object pronouns.

	DISJUNCTIVE PRONOUNS	
SINGULAR		
1st PERSON	moi	*me*
2nd PERSON	toi	*you*
3rd PERSON	lui, elle	*him, her, it*
PLURAL		
1st PERSON	nous	*us*
2nd PERSON	vous	*you (men & women)*
3rd PERSON	eux, elles	*them (men & women)*

As in English, disjunctive pronouns are used in short answers when the identity of the person we refer to is obvious from the context.

Who is coming? **Us.**
Qui vient ? **Nous.**

Who are you leaving with? **Her.**
Avec qui partez-vous ? **Elle.**
  elle → fem. sing.

With whom are you going on holiday? **Him.**
Avec qui partez-vous en vacances ? **Lui.**
  lui → masc. sing.

In French, disjunctive pronouns are also used:

- **Before a subject pronoun** to replace the emphasis used in English or to contrast one subject with another:

    *What do you do for work? **I** work in a law firm, **she** works in a restaurant.*
    Que faites-vous comme travail ? **Moi, je** travaille dans un cabinet d'avocats. **Elle, elle** travaille dans un restaurant.
    moi, je → disjunctive pronoun + subject pronoun
    elle, elle → disjunctive pronoun + subject pronoun

- **As direct and indirect objects** of the 1st and 2nd person singular of verbs in the affirmative imperative (see *The Imperative*):

    *Pass **her** the salt.*
    Passe-**lui** le sel.

    Get up.
    Lève-**toi**.

- **As objects of a preposition.** Remember, if the pronoun follows the preposition **à** it is an indirect object and takes an indirect object pronoun, not a disjunctive pronoun:

    Is the cake for Marie-Jeanne?
    *No, it's **for me**.*
    *No, it's **for you**.*
    *No, it's **for us**.*
    1. Identify the verb: to be
    2. What is the French equivalent: **être**
    3. Is the French verb followed by a preposition: yes.
    4. What preposition: **pour** *(for)*
    5. Function of pronoun in French: object of preposition
    6. Selection: **moi, toi (vous), nous**

    Est-ce que le gâteau est pour Marie-Jeanne ?
    Non, il est **pour moi.**
    Non, il est **pour toi (vous).**
    Non, il est **pour nous.**

    *Is the cat **with** Carole? Yes, it is **with her**.*
    1. Identify the verb: to be
    2. What is the French equivalent: **être**
    3. Is the French verb followed by a preposition: yes
    4. What preposition: **avec** *(with)*
    5. Function of pronoun in French: object of preposition

    6. Gender of antecedent: feminine *(Carole)*
    7. Selection: **elle**

Est-ce que le chat est **avec** Carole ? Oui, il est **avec elle.**

*Is the dog **with** Martin? Yes, it is **with** him.*
    1 - 5. See above.
    6. Gender of antecedent: masculine (Martin)
    7. Selection: **lui**

Est-ce que le chien est **avec** Martin ? Oui, il est **avec lui.**

*Did you receive an invitation from Sarah and Mathieu? Yes, we have received an invitation **from them.***
    1. Identify the verb: to receive
    2. What is the French equivalent: **recevoir**
    3. Is the French verb followed by a preposition: yes
    4. What preposition: **de** *(from)*
    5. Function of pronoun in French: object of preposition
    6. Gender of antecedent: masculine *(Sarah and Mathieu)*
    7. Selection: **eux**

Avez-vous reçu une invitation de Sarah et Mathieu ? Oui, nous avons reçu une invitation **d'eux.**

*Did you buy a present for Camille and Clara? No, I did not buy a gift **for them.***
    1. Identify the verb: to buy
    2. What is the French equivalent: **acheter**
    3. Is the French verb followed by a preposition: yes
    4. What preposition: **pour** *(for)*
    5. Function of pronoun in French: object of preposition
    6. Gender of antecedent: feminine *(Camille and Clara)*
    7. Selection: **elles**

As-tu acheté un cadeau pour Camille et Clara ? Non, je n'ai pas acheté de cadeau **pour elles.**

Exception: When *it* or *them* (referring to a thing or an idea) are objects of the preposition **de** *(of)*, the pronoun **en** is used.

*Traveling is his passion. He talks about **it** often.*
    1. Identify the verb: to talk
    2. What is the French equivalent: **parler**
    3. Is the French verb followed by **de**: yes
    4. Function of pronoun in French: object of preposition *de*
    5. Type of antecedent: traveling (hobby)
    6. Selection: **en** (replaces *de* + pronoun)

Voyager est sa passion. Il **en** parle souvent.

*We had dogs when we were growing up. I remember **them**.*
1. Identify the verb: to remember
2. What is the French equivalent: **se souvenir**
3. Is the French verb followed by **de**: yes
4. Function of pronoun in French: object of preposition *de*
5. Type of antecedent: **dogs** (thing)
6. Selection: **en** (replaces **de** + pronoun)

Nous avions des chiens en grandissant. Je m'**en** souviens.

Careful – Make sure you establish the correct type of object for the French verb, which might not always be the same as the object used with the English verb (see *Relationship of a Verb to Its Object* within the *Objects* chapter).

Summary of French Object Pronouns

DO → Direct object of the French verb
IO → Indirect object of the French verb
OP → Object of a preposition of the French verb
DP → Disjunctive pronoun
Imp. → Affirmative imperative

ME – 1st pers. sing.
   1. DO/IO → me
      DO: *She calls **me**.* → Elle **m'**appelle.
      IO: *He gives **me** a gift.* → Il **me** donne un cadeau.

   2. OP/DP → moi
      OP: *She is sitting next to **me**.* → Elle est assise à côté de **moi**.
      Imp. + DO → DP: *Help **me**.* → Aide-**moi**.
      Imp. + IO → DP: *Write to **me**.* → Écris-**moi**.
      Imp. + OP/DP: *Come with **me**.* → Viens avec **moi**.

YOU – 2nd pers. sing./pl.
   1. Familiar sing.
     • **DO/IO → te**
        DO: *I know **you**.* → Je **te** connais.
        IO: *She sent **you** a letter.* → Elle **t'**a envoyé une lettre.
     • **OP/DP → toi**
        OP: *They are walking with **you**.* → Ils marchent avec **toi**.
        Imp. + DO → DP: *Wake up.* → Réveille-**toi**.

   2. Familiar pl. and formal sing. & pl. → vous

DO: *She helps **you**.* → Elle **vous** aide.
IO: *He sends **you** an email.* → Il **vous** envoie un email.
OP: *They are laughing at **you**.* → Elles se moquent de **vous**.
Imp. + DO → DP: *Wake up.* → Réveillez-**vous**.

HIM – 3rd pers. sing.
1. DO → le
DO: *I know **him**.* → Je **le** connais.
Imp. + DO: *Find **him**.* → Trouve-**le**.

2. IO/OP → lui
IO: *She gives **him** a gift.* → Elle **lui** donne un cadeau.
OP: *They are playing with **him**.* → Ils jouent avec **lui**.
Imp. + IO: *Tell **him**.* → Dis-**lui**.

HER – 3rd pers. sing.
1. DO → la
DO: *I admire **her**.* → Je l'admire.
Imp. + DO: *Help **her**.* → Aidez-**la**.

2. IO → lui
IO: *He sends **her** a message.* → Il **lui** envoie un message.
Imp. + IO: *Give **her** the book.* → Donne-**lui** le livre.

3. OP → elle
OP: *I went to the cinema with **her**.* → J'ai été au cinéma avec **elle**.

IT – 3rd pers. sing.
1. DO
- **masc. antecedent → le**
  DO: *He likes **it**.* → Il l'aime bien. *(le verre)*
  Imp. + DO: *Find **it**.* → Trouve-**le**.
- **fem. antecedent → la**
  DO: *She wants **it**.* → Elle **la** veut. *(l'assiette)*
  Imp. + DO: *Save **it**.* → Sauve-**la**.

2. IO → y
*She thinks about **it**.* → Elle **y** pense. *(penser à)*

3. OP + de → en
*I dream of **it**.* → J'**en** rêve.

US – 1st pers. pl. → nous
DO: *They invited **us**.* → Ils **nous** ont invités.

IO: *She sent **us** a parcel.* → Elle **nous** a envoyé un colis.
OP: *You walk with **us**.* → Tu marches avec **nous**.
Imp. + DO: *Follow **us**.* → Suivez-**nous**.

THEM – 3rd pers. pl.

1. **DO (antecedent a person/thing) → les**
   DO: *She calls **them**.* → Elle **les** appelle.
   Imp. + DO: *Stop **them**.* → Arrêtez-**les**.

2. **IO (antecedent a person) → leur**
   IO: *He bought **them** gifts.* → Il **leur** a acheté des cadeaux.
   Imp. + IO: *Explain to **them**.* → Explique-**leur**.

3. **IO (antecedent a thing) → y**
   *He thinks of **it**.* → Il **y** pense.

4. **OP including de (antecedent a person)**
   - masc. antecedent → eux
     *She is working with **them** (men).* → Elle travaille avec **eux**.
     Imp. + OP: *Work with **them**.* → Travaille avec **eux**.
     *She works for **them**.* → Elle travaille pour **eux**.
   - fem. antecedent → elles
     *He is working with **them** (women).* → Il travaille avec **elles**.
     Imp. + OP: *Work with **them**.* → Travaille avec **elles**.
     *He works for **them**.* → Il travaille pour **elles**.

5. **OP de (antecedent a thing) → en**
   *He dreams about **them** (his trips).* → Il **en** rêve.

FRENCH FACT: LEXICON

The French language has around 1.5 million words, making it one of the largest lexicons in the world. It is also known for being one of the most challenging languages to master.

Chapter 40: Reflexive Pronouns and Verbs

> **ILLUSTRATIVE EXAMPLE**
>
> English: *After waking up early, she dresses and admires **herself** in the mirror before going for a run to enjoy **herself** in the fresh morning air.*
>
> French: *Après **s'être réveillée** tôt, elle **s'habille** et **s'admire** dans le miroir avant d'aller courir pour **se détendre** dans l'air frais du matin.*

A **Reflexive Verb** is a verb that is accompanied by a pronoun, called a **Reflexive Pronoun**, which reflects the action of the verb back to the subject.

> I hurt *myself* while rock climbing.
> I → subject = reflexive pronoun → same person
> hurt myself → reflexive verb

In English
Many regular verbs can take on a reflexive meaning by adding a reflexive pronoun.

> We *enjoyed* the party.
> enjoyed → regular verb
>
> We *enjoyed* ourselves at the party.
> enjoyed ourselves → verb + reflexive pronoun

Reflexive pronouns end with *-self* in the singular and *-selves* in the plural.

	SUBJECT PRONOUN +	VERB +	REFLEXIVE PRONOUN
SINGULAR			
1st PERSON	I	wash	myself
2nd PERSON	you	wash	yourself
3rd PERSON	he, she, it	washes	himself, herself, itself
PLURAL			
1st PERSON	we	wash	ourselves
2nd PERSON	you	wash	yourselves
3rd PERSON	they	wash	themselves

As the subject changes, so does the reflexive pronoun, because they both refer to the same person or object.

> I taught *myself* how to sew.
> Manon and Jeremy challenged *themselves* to run a race.

Although *you* applies to both the singular and plural, the reflexive pronouns change form. *Yourself* is used when talking about one person (singular), and *yourselves* for more than one (plural).

> Marion, did you cut *yourself*?
> You congratulated *yourselves* on your historic win.

Reflexive verbs can be in any tense: *I remind myself, I reminded myself, I will remind myself,* etc.

In French

As in English, reflexive verbs, also called **les Verbes Réfléchis** or **les Verbes Pronominaux**, are formed with a verb and a reflexive pronoun.

Here are the French reflexive pronouns:

SINGULAR		
1st PERSON	me	*myself*
2nd PERSON	te	*yourself*
3rd PERSON	se	*himself, herself, itself*
PLURAL		
1st PERSON	nous	*ourselves*
2nd PERSON	vous	*yourself, yourselves*
3rd PERSON	se	*themselves*

In the dictionary, reflexive verbs are listed under the regular verb. For instance, under **brosser** *(to brush)* you will also find **se brosser** *(to brush oneself)*.

Look at the conjugation of **se brosser.** Notice two things:
1. As in English, for conjugations, the reflexive pronoun changes depending on the person.
2. Unlike in English, the reflexive pronoun is placed before the verb.

	SUBJECT PRONOUN +	REFLEXIVE PRONOUN +	VERB
SINGULAR			
1st PERSON	je	me	brosse
2nd PERSON	tu	te	brosses
3rd PERSON	il, elle, on	se	brosse
PLURAL			
1st PERSON	nous	nous	brossons
2nd PERSON	vous	vous	brossez
3rd PERSON	ils, elles	se	brossent

Reflexive verbs can be conjugated in all tenses. The subject and reflexive pronouns stay the same, no matter which tense the verb uses. For example, **je me brosserai** (*future*); **je me suis brossé** (*past tense*). In compound tenses, reflexive verbs are conjugated with the auxiliary verb **être**, but the rules of agreement of the past participle of reflexive verbs are different from those for regular verbs.

Regular verbs that use the auxiliary **être** in compound tenses can't become reflexive. But regular verbs that use **avoir** in compound tenses can become reflexive when we add **être** as an auxiliary.

REGULAR VERB	REFLEXIVE VERB
Il **a coupé** le gâteau	Il **s'est coupé** en cuisinant
*He **cut** the cake*	*He **cut himself** while cooking*
Myriam **a acheté** une montre	Myriam **s'est achetée** une montre
*Myriam **bought** a watch*	*Myriam **bought herself** a watch*
Jean et Colette **ont fait** le dîner	Jean et Colette **se sont fait** des habits
*Jean and Colette **made** dinner*	*Jean and Colette **made themselves** some clothes*

Reflexive verbs are common in French. There are many expressions that are not reflexive in English, but whose French equivalent are. You will have to memorize these idiomatic expressions.

to get up	se lever (*to get oneself up*)
to go to bed	se coucher (*to put oneself to bed*)
to wake up	se réveiller (*to wake oneself up*)

to be bored	s'ennuyer *(to bore oneself)*
to have a good time	s'amuser *(to amuse oneself)*
to make a mistake	se tromper *(to mistake oneself)*
to stop	s'arrêter *(to stop oneself)*
to take a walk	se promener *(to walk oneself)*

In all the examples above, the French reflexive pronouns have the same meaning to the English reflexive pronouns (*myself, yourself, himself*, etc.). That is not always the case. French reflexive pronouns can also indicate reciprocal action.

Reciprocal Action

In English
English uses a regular verb followed by the expression *each other* to express reciprocal action (an action between two or more persons, or things).

> My mom and dad yelled at *each other*.
>> The expression *each other* tells us that the action of yelling was reciprocal (my mom yelled at my dad, and my dad yelled at my mom).

> My neighbors see *each other* every morning.
>> The expression *each other* tells us that the action of seeing is reciprocal (my various neighbors see one another every morning).

Since reciprocal verbs require the involvement of more than one person or thing, the verb is always plural.

In French
French uses reflexive pronouns to express an action that is reciprocal.

> Ma mère et mon père **se** criaient dessus.
> *My mom and dad yelled at **each other**.*

> Mes voisins **se** voient tous les matins.
> *My neighbors see **each other** every morning.*

Sometimes, the meaning of a French reflexive pronoun can be ambiguous.

> Les étudiants **se parlent.**

*The students **talk to themselves**. → REFLEXIVE*
*The students **talk to each other**. → RECIPROCAL*

One way to avoid confusion, and to clearly indicate that the meaning is reciprocal rather than reflexive, is to add an expression equivalent to *each other*, which is **l'un l'autre** *(singular)* or **les uns les autres** *(plural)*.

>Le chien et le chat se regardent **l'un l'autre.**
>>chien → singular
>>chat → singular
>>l'un l'autre → singular
>
>*The dog and the cat look at **each other**.*
>
>Les étudiants se parlent **les uns les autres.**
>>étudiants → plural
>>les uns les autres → plural
>
>*The students talk to **each other**.*

FRENCH FACT: TONGUE TWISTERS
French has some challenging tongue twisters, like **les chaussettes de l'archiduchesse sont-elles sèches, archi-sèches ?** *(Are the archduchess's socks dry, very dry?)*. Practicing these can improve pronunciation and fluency, and don't fret as even native French speakers struggle to say them!

CHAPTER 41: POSSESSIVE PRONOUNS

> **ILLUSTRATIVE EXAMPLE**
>
> English: Her dog's favorite toy is **his** squeaky ball, but **mine** prefers **his** chew bone.
>
> French: Le jouet préféré de **son** chien est **sa** balle qui couine, mais **le mien** préfère **son** os à mâcher.

A **Possessive Pronoun** is a word that replaces a noun and indicates the possessor of that noun. The word possessive comes from *possess*, to own.

> Whose shoes are these? They're his.
> *His* replaces the noun *shoes*, the object possessed, and shows who possesses it *(him)*.

In English
Here is a list of the possessive pronouns:

SINGULAR POSSESSOR		
1st PERSON		mine
2nd PERSON		yours
3rd PERSON	masculine, feminine	his, hers
PLURAL POSSESSOR		
1st PERSON		ours
2nd PERSON		yours
3rd PERSON		theirs

Possessive pronouns refer to the possessor, not to the object possessed.

> My dress is blue; what color is Clara's? *Hers* is black.
> hers → 3rd pers. fem. sing.

> Catherine's dress is blue; what color is yours? *Mine* is black.
> mine → 1st pers. sing.
> Although the object possessed is the same *(dress)*, different possessive pronouns *(hers and mine)* are used because the possessors are different *(Catherine and me)*.

> Is it Maxime's bag? Yes, it is *his*.

Are those Maxime's things? Yes, they are *his*.

> Although the objects possessed are different *(bag* and *things)*, the same possessive pronoun *(his)* is used because the possessor is the same *(Maxime)*.

In French

Like in English, French possessive pronouns refer to the possessor. However, unlike English and like all French pronouns, they also agree in gender and number with their **antecedent** (with the person or thing possessed). In addition, the possessive pronoun is preceded by a definite article that also agrees in gender and number with the antecedent.

Let's look at French possessive pronouns to see how they are formed. We have divided the French possessive pronouns into two groups.

Singular Possessor

1st, 2nd and 3rd pers. sing.: *mine, yours* (tu-form), *his/hers*.

Each of these possessive pronouns has four forms depending on the gender and number of the antecedent. To choose the proper form follow these steps.

> 1. Indicate the possessor. This will be shown by the first letter of the possessive pronoun (they are the same initial letters as the possessive adjectives, see *Possessive Adjectives*)

mine	*m-*
yours (tu form)	*t-*
his	*-s*
hers	

> 2. Establish the gender and number of the antecedent.
>
> 3. Choose the definite article and the ending that corresponds to the antecedent's gender and number.
>
> - Noun possessed is masculine singular → **le** + first letter of the possessor + **-ien**

À qui est ce **sac** ? [masc. sing.]	C'est **le mien**
	C'est **le tien**
	C'est **le sien**
Whose **bag** is that?	It is **mine**
	It is **yours**
	It is **his, hers**

- Noun possessed is feminine singular → **la** + first letter of the possessor + **-ienne**

À qui est cette **robe** ? [fem. sing.]	C'est **la mienne**
	C'est **la tienne**
	C'est **la sienne**
Whose **dress** is that?	It is **mine**
	It is **yours**
	It is **his, hers**

- Noun possessed is masculine plural → **les** + first letter of the possessor +**-iens**

À qui sont ces **vêtements** ? [masc. pl.]	C'est **les miens**.
	C'est **les tiens**.
	C'est **les siens**.
Whose **clothes** are those?	They are **mine**.
	They are **yours**.
	They are **his, hers**.

- Noun possessed is feminine plural → **les** + first letter of the possessor + **-iennes**

A qui sont ces **affaires** ? [fem. pl.]	C'est **les miennes**
	C'est **les tiennes**
	C'est **les siennes**

Whose **things** are those?	They are **mine**
	They are **yours**
	They are **his, hers**

4. Select the proper form according to the two steps above.

Let's apply these steps to some examples.

*Charles is putting away his things. Claude is putting away **hers**.*
1. Possessor: hers (familiar) → 3rd pers. sing. → **s-**
2. Antecedent: **affaires** *(things)* → feminine plural
3. Add definite article & ending: **les** + **s-** + **-iennes**

Charles range ses affaires. Claude range **les siennes.**

*Can I borrow your bag? No, but you can borrow **his**.*
1. Possessor: his → 3rd pers. sing. → **s-**
2. Antecedent: **sac** *(bag)* → masculine singular
3. Add definite article & ending: **le** + **s-** + **-ien**

Puis-je emprunter ton sac ? Non, mais tu peux emprunter **le sien.**

Plural Possessor

1st, 2nd and 3rd pers. pl.: *ours, yours* (vous-form), *theirs*.

Each of these possessive pronouns has a singular form and a plural form, depending on the number of the antecedent (the noun they refer to). The definite article before the pronoun also agrees in gender and number of the noun. To choose the proper form, follow these steps:

1. Indicate the possessor.

ours	**nôtre**
yours	**vôtre**
theirs	**leur**

2. Establish the gender and number of the antecedent.
3. Choose the definite article that corresponds to the antecedent's gender and number.
4. If the antecedent is plural, add an *s* to the possessive pronoun.

Let's apply these steps to some examples.

*He paid for my meal. Did he pay for **yours**?*
1. Possessor: yours (formal) → 2nd pers. pl. → **vôtre**
2. Antecedent: **repas** *(meal)* → masculine singular → **le**
3. Selection: **le vôtre**

Il a payé mon repas. A-t-il payé **le vôtre** ?

*I forgot my textbooks but Daniel and Jonathan brought **theirs**.*
1. Possessor: theirs → 3rd pers. pl. → **leur**
2. Antecedent: **manuels scolaires** *(textbooks)* → masculine plural → **les**
3. Make possessive pronoun plural: **les** + **leur** + **s**

J'ai oublié mes manuels scolaires mais Daniel et Jonathan ont amené **les leurs.**

Although **vôtre** is classified as second person plural, it can refer to just one person when used as a formal form of address.

Summary

Here is a chart you can use as a reference.

SINGULAR POSSESSOR	NOUN POSSESSED	
	SINGULAR	PLURAL
mine - *masc. fem.*	le mien, la mienne	les miens, les miennes
yours (tu-form) - *masc. fem.*	le tien, la tienne	les tiens, les tiennes
his, hers - *masc. fem.*	le sien, la sienne	les siens, les siennes
PLURAL POSSESSOR	NOUN POSSESSED	
	SINGULAR	PLURAL
ours - *masc. fem.*	le nôtre, la nôtre	les nôtres
yours (vous-form) - *masc. fem.*	le vôtre, la vôtre	les vôtres
theirs - *masc. fem.*	la leur, le leur	les leurs

STUDY TIPS: POSSESSIVE PRONOUNS

1. You can easily establish a pattern by following our instructions above under *Singular Possessors* and *Plural Possessors*.
2. Note the circumflex accent over the *o* in **nôtre** and **vôtre** which, along with the definite article, distinguishes these plural possessive pronouns from the plural forms of the possessive adjective **notre** and **votre** (see *Possessive Adjectives*).

Practice

1. You can use the same selection of noun flashcards you used to practice possessive adjectives.

2. Look at the French side and go through the cards replacing the nouns with the correct form of the possessive pronoun. Concentrate on the singular forms **le mien, le tien, le sien** as they are the forms that change.

un magasin	*store, shop*
le mien, le tien, le sien	*mine, yours, his/hers*
une chambre	*bedroom*
la mienne, la tienne, la sienne	*mine, yours, his/hers*

3. Write short questions in French requiring an answer with a possessive pronoun.

Est-ce que c'est ton téléphone ?	*Is that your phone?*
Oui, c'est le mien	*Yes, it is mine*
Est-ce que ce sont tes affaires ?	*Are those your things?*
Oui, ce sont les miennes	*Yes, they are mine*

4. Give negative answers to the questions you wrote under point 3 so that the answer will require a different possessive pronoun from the one given above.

Est-ce que c'est ton téléphone?	*Is that your phone?*
Non, c'est le sien	*No, it's hers/his*
Est-ce que ce sont tes affaires ?	*Are those your things?*
Non, ce sont les vôtres	*No, they are yours*

Flashcards

1. To practice, create one card per person (1st, 2nd, and 3rd person singular and plural) with an example of the different forms.

>le mien, la mienne, les miens, les miennes → *mine*
>le tien, la tienne, les tiens, les tiennes → *yours*
>etc.

2. On the cards for the 3rd person singular and plural, to reinforce the fact that *his* or *hers* can be either **le sien, la sienne, les siens, les siennes**, write French questions requiring answers equivalent to *his* and *hers*.

Est-ce que c'est l'ordinateur de Camille/Michel ?	*Is it Camille/ Michel's computer?*
Oui, c'est le sien	*Yes, it's hers/his*
Est-ce que ce sont les affaires de Camille/Michel ?	*Are they Camille/ Michel's things?*
Oui, ce sont les siennes	*Yes, they're hers/his*
Est-ce que ce sont les habits de Camille/Michel ?	Are they Camille/ Michel's clothes?
Oui, ce sont les siens	Yes, they're hers/his

Chapter 42: Interrogative Pronouns

> **ILLUSTRATIVE EXAMPLE**
>
> English: **Who** is coming to the party, and **what** should we bring for them? Do you remember **whom** we are going with?
>
> French: **Qui est-ce qui** vient à la fête, et **que** devrions-nous apporter pour eux ? Te souviens-tu **avec qui** nous allons ?

An **Interrogative Pronoun** is a word that replaces a noun and introduces a question. The word interrogative comes from *interrogate*, to question.

    Who is invited to the wedding?
        who → replaces a person

    What did you make for dinner?
        what → replaces a thing

In English and French, different interrogative pronouns are used for people (humans, animals) and things (objects, ideas). The form of the interrogative pronouns also changes based on their function in the sentence: subject, direct object, indirect object, or object of a preposition. We'll look at each function separately.

Subject
(See *Subjects*)

In English
A different interrogative pronoun is used depending on whether it refers to a person or a thing.

    PERSON → who
    Who is coming?
        who → subject
        is → verb 3rd. pers. sing.

    THING → what
    What is in the box?
        what → subject
        is → verb 3rd. pers. sing.

An interrogative pronoun used as a subject is followed by a verb in the 3rd person singular.

In French
Same as in English, a different interrogative pronoun is used depending on whether it refers to a person or a thing.

PERSON → qui + verb or **qui est-ce qui** + verb
    Qui vient ?
    Qui est-ce qui vient ?
        vient → verb 3rd. pers. sing.
    Who is coming?

THING → Qu'est-ce qui + verb
    Qu'est-ce qui se trouve dans la boîte ?
        se trouve → verb 3rd. pers. sing.
    What is in the box?

Same as in English, an interrogative pronoun used as a subject is followed by a verb in the 3rd person singular.

Direct Object
(See *Objects*)

In English
A different interrogative pronoun is used depending on whether it refers to a person or a thing.

PERSON → whom
    Whom are you coming with?
        whom → direct object
        you → subject
        In spoken English, *whom* is often replaced by *who* (ex: *Who are you coming with?*). Only by analyzing the sentence will you be able to establish the function of the interrogative pronoun.

THING → what
    What did you buy?
        what → direct object
        you → subject

In French
No matter the function of the French interrogative pronoun, forms with **est-ce que** keep the usual word order: subject (noun or pronoun) + verb. The other forms use an inverted order: verb + subject pronoun (this is rarely used with a subject noun).

Same as in English, a different interrogative pronoun is used depending on whether it refers to a person or a thing.

PERSON → **qui est-ce que** + subject + verb *or* **qui** + verb + subject pronoun

> **Qui est-ce que** vous appelez ?
> subject → vous
> verb → appelez
> **Qui** appelez-vous ?
> appelez → verb
> vous → subject pronoun
> **Who(m)** *are you calling?*

THING → **qu'est-ce que** + subject + verb *or* **que** + verb + subject pronoun

> **Qu'est-ce que** tu cherches ?
> tu → subject
> cherches → verb
> **Que** cherches-tu ?
> cherches → verb
> tu → subject pronoun
> **What** *are you looking for?*

Indirect Object and Object of a Preposition
(See *Objects*)

In English
The same form of the interrogative pronoun is used as an indirect object and as an object of a preposition. However, a different interrogative pronoun is used depending on whether it refers to a person or a thing.

PERSON → **whom, who** (see **restructuring sentences** below)
> *Who are you talking to?* → *To whom are you talking?*
> whom → indirect object

> *Who did you meet with?* → *With whom did you meet?*
> whom → indirect object

THING → what
>   *What* did you clean it *with*? → *With what* did you clean it?
>   >   what → object of a preposition

Restructuring Sentences with Dangling Prepositions

It is difficult to identify an English interrogative pronoun functioning as an indirect object or as an object of a preposition for two reasons:

1. The interrogative pronoun is often separated from the preposition it goes with. In this case, the preposition is called a **Dangling Preposition.**
2. In spoken English the direct object whom is often replaced by *who*.

> *Who(m)* did you go *with*?
> > who(m) → interrogative pronoun
> > with → dangling preposition
>
> *Who(m)* did you buy it *for*?
> > who(m) → interrogative pronoun
> > for → dangling preposition

To figure out if an interrogative pronoun is an indirect object or an object of a preposition, you need to change the sentence structure so the preposition is placed before the interrogative pronoun. This restructuring makes it simpler to identify the pronoun's function and sets up the word order for the French sentence.

The following sentences have been restructured to avoid a dangling preposition.

> *Who* is the gift *for*?
> > who → interrogative pronoun
> > for → dangling preposition
>
> *For whom* is the gift?
> > for whom → indirect object
>
> *Who* did you do this *for*?
> > who → interrogative pronoun
> > for → dangling preposition
>
> *For whom* did you do this?
> > for whom → indirect object
>
> *Who* are you living *with*?
> > who → interrogative pronoun
> > with → dangling preposition
>
> *With whom* are you living?
> > with whom → object of the preposition *with*

What did you clean it *with*?
> what → interrogative pronoun
> with → dangling preposition

With what did you clean it?
> with what → object of the preposition *with*

In French

As in English, the same form of the interrogative pronoun is used as an indirect object (always preceded by the preposition **à**) and as an object of a preposition (always preceded by a preposition other than **à**). As in English, a different interrogative pronoun is used depending on whether it refers to a person or a thing.

PERSON → preposition + **qui est-ce que** + subject + verb or preposition + **qui** + verb + subject pronoun

> **À qui est-ce que** vous envoyez la lettre ?
> > vous envoyez → subject + verb
>
> **À qui** envoyez-vous la lettre ?
> > envoyez-vous → verb + subject pronoun
>
> ***To whom*** *are you sending the letter?* (***Who*** *are you sending the letter* ***to?***)
> > to whom → indirect object

> **Avec qui est-ce que** tu voyages ?
> > tu voyages → subject + verb
>
> **Avec qui** voyages-tu ?
> > voyages-tu → verb + subject pronoun
>
> ***With whom*** *are you traveling?* (***Who*** *are you traveling* ***with?***)
> > with whom → object of preposition *with*

THING → preposition + **quoi est-ce que** + subject + verb or preposition + **quoi** + verb + subject pronoun

> **À quoi est-ce que** tu fais attention ?
> > tu fais attention → subject + verb
>
> **À quoi** fais-tu attention ?
> > fais-tu attention → verb + subject pronoun
>
> ***To what*** *are you paying attention?* (***What*** *are you paying attention* ***to?***)
> > to what → indirect object

> **Avec quoi est-ce** que tu cuisines ?
> > tu cuisines → subject + verb
>
> **Avec quoi** cuisines-tu ?
> > cuisines-tu → verb + subject pronoun

***With what** are you cooking? (**What** are you cooking **with**?)*
  with what → object of preposition *with*

Careful – Remember: some French verbs take direct objects, while the equivalent verbs in English take an indirect object, and inversely (see *Relationship of a Verb to Its Object* within the *Objects* chapter). You must always determine the function of the pronoun in French.

Summary

To choose the correct form of French interrogative pronouns, proceed with the following three steps:

1. Determine the function of the interrogative pronoun in the French sentence.
2. Establish whether the pronoun refers to a person or a thing.
3. Refer to the chart below.

	SUBJECT	DIRECT OBJECT	INDIRECT OBJECT & OBJECT OF A PREPOSITION
PERSON	who	who(m)	preposition + who(m)
	qui est-ce qui	qui est-ce que	prép + qui est-ce que
	qui est-ce qui	qui (+ inversion)	prép + qui (+ inversion)
THING	what	what	preposition + what
	qu'est-ce qui	qu'est-ce que	prép + quoi est-ce que
		que (+ inversion)	prép + quoi (+ inversion)

Which (one), Which (ones)

There is another interrogative pronoun that we will examine because it does not follow the same pattern as the ones above.

In English

Which (one) and *which (ones)* are used in questions that request the selection of one (*which one*, singular) or more (*which ones*, plural) items from a mentioned group. Usually, *one* and *ones* are left out. These interrogative pronouns can refer to both people and things. They don't change based on their role in the sentence and can be used as subjects, direct objects, indirect objects, or objects of a preposition.

We have several books. *Which* one would you like?
    several books → group mentioned
    which one → singular subject

There are many desserts. *Which one* are you ordering?
    many desserts → group mentioned
    which one → singular direct object

We saw many paintings. *Which ones* were your favorite?
    many paintings → group mentioned
    which ones → plural direct object

There are so many toys. *Which ones* does Jacques play *with*?
    many toys → group mentioned
    ones → plural object of preposition *with*

In French

Just like in English, these interrogative pronouns do not change according to function. However, their form changes in two ways:

1. Their gender depends on the gender of their **antecedent** (the noun which the pronoun refers to).
2. Their number depends on whether you want to say **which one** (singular) or **which ones** (plural).

		MASCULINE	FEMININE
SINGULAR	which (one)	lequel	laquelle
PLURAL	which (ones)	lesquels	lesquelles

To choose the proper form, follow these steps:
1. Find the antecedent of *which*.
2. Determine the gender of the antecedent.
3. Do you wish to say *which one* (singular) or *which ones* (plural)?
4. Select the correct French form from the chart above.

Let's apply these steps to some examples.

*We have plenty of films. **Which one** would you like to watch?*
1. Antecedent: films
2. Gender: **films** *(films)* → masculine
3. Number: one → singular
4. Selection: masculine singular → **lequel**

Nous avons beaucoup de films. **Lequel** voudriez-vous regarder ?

They sell many nice dresses. **Which one** *are you buying?*
1. Antecedent: dresses
2. Gender: **robes** *(dresses)* → feminine
3. Number: one → singular
4. Selection: feminine singular → **laquelle**

Ils vendent beaucoup de belles robes. **Laquelle** vas-tu acheter ?

We saw many paintings. **Which ones** *were your favorite?*
1. Antecedent: paintings
2. Gender: **tableaux** *(paintings)* → masculine
3. Number: ones → plural
4. Selection: masculine plural → **lesquels**

Nous avons vu beaucoup de tableaux. **Lesquels** étaient tes préférés ?

There are different universities; **which ones** *did you apply* **to?** → *There are different universities;* **to which ones** *did you apply?*
1. Antecedent: universities
2. Gender: **universités** *(universities)* → feminine
3. Number: ones → plural.
4. Selection: feminine plural → **à** + **lesquelles** → **auxquelles**

Il y a des universités différentes ; **auxquelles** as-tu postulé ?

We received many comments. **Which one** *would you like to talk about first?* → *We received many comments.* **About which one** *would you like to talk first?*
1. Antecedent: comments
2. Gender: **commentaires** *(comments)* → masculine
3. Number: one → singular
4. Selection: masculine singular → **de** (*about*) + **lequel** → **duquel**

Nous avons reçu beaucoup de commentaires. **Duquel** voulez-vous parler en premier ?

STUDY TIPS: INTERROGATIVE PRONOUNS

Pattern

1. Look for a pattern that distinguishes the interrogative pronouns referring to people from those referring to things.
   - **PEOPLE** → interrogative pronouns referring to people start with **qui** or preposition + **qui** (*Avec qui est-ce que tu travailles ?*)
   - **THINGS** → interrogative pronouns referring to things start with **qu'** or preposition + **quoi** (*Avec quoi est-ce que tu cuisines ?*)

PERSON	Qui / Prep. + qui	est-ce	qui	**SUBJECT**
THING	Qu' / Prep. + quoi		que/ qu'	**OBJECT**

2. Look for a pattern that distinguishes interrogative pronouns functioning as subjects from those functioning as objects.
- **SUBJECTS** → interrogative pronoun subjects end in **qui**.
- **OBJECTS** → interrogative pronoun objects end in **que (qui)**.

3. To learn the inversion forms, refer to the chapter *Declarative* and *Interrogative Sentences*. Remember that after the beginning **qui, qu'** or *preposition +* **qui/quoi,** you invert the subject pronoun and verb *(Avec qui travailles-tu ?, Avec quoi cuisinez-vous ?)*. **EXCEPTION**: If **qui** is the subject, it is followed by a verb *(Qui mange ?, Qui est-ce qui mange ?)*.

Practice
1. On a blank piece of paper write questions using the various French forms.
2. Write French sentences answering *who* and *what* questions. Then write a series of questions in French and answer them.

SENTENCE: Marion cuisine le déjeuner avec des ustensiles de cuisine.

QUESTION: Qui cuisine le déjeuner ?
ANSWER: Marion cuisine le déjeuner.

QUESTION: Qu'est-ce que Marion cuisine ?
ANSWER: Elle cuisine le déjeuner.

QUESTION: Avec quoi est-ce qu'elle cuisine le déjeuner ?
ANSWER: Elle cuisine le déjeuner avec des ustensiles de cuisine.

Flashcards
To practice and study, create a card with a short question illustrating each form.

Chapter 43: Relative Pronouns

> **ILLUSTRATIVE EXAMPLE**
>
> <u>English:</u> *I borrowed the book **that** you had previously recommended to me from the library. It was a great read!*
>
> <u>French:</u> *J'ai emprunté le livre, **que** tu m'avais recommandé précédemment, à la bibliothèque. C'était une excellente lecture !*

A **Relative Pronoun** is a word used at the beginning of a clause that gives additional information about someone or something previously mentioned.

> I am eating the cake *that* Julie baked this afternoon.
> that Julie baked this afternoon → relative clause providing additional information about the cake

A relative pronoun serves two purposes:

1. It modifies a noun previously mentioned. The noun to which it refers is called the **Antecedent**.

> We saw the man *who* committed the crime.
> man → antecedent of the relative pronoun *who*

2. It introduces a **Relative Clause**, which is a group of words that has a subject and a verb but can't stand alone because it doesn't express a complete thought. Instead, it's dependent on another part of the sentence called the **Main Clause**, which can stand alone as a complete sentence and thought. Throughout the chapter, you'll see relative clauses underlined, while the other words make up the main clause.

> The man <u>who committed the crime</u> is mentally ill.
> man → subject
> who → subject
> committed → verb
> is → verb

Relative clauses are very common. They allow us to combine in a single sentence two thoughts that have a common element.

SENTENCE A	I married a man.
SENTENCE B	He is a police officer.
COMBINED	I married a man <u>who is a police officer</u>.

A relative pronoun can have different functions in a relative clause: it can be the subject, direct object, indirect object, object of a preposition, or a possessive relative pronoun. The choice of relative pronoun for each function usually depends on whether it refers to a person (human or animal) or a thing (object or idea).

Some forms are more common in spoken English, others in formal or written English.

I. Relative Pronoun as Subject
(See *Subjects*)

In English
Relative pronouns functioning as subjects in a relative clause are always used in spoken and written English. The verb agrees with the antecedent of the relative pronoun. The choice of the relative pronoun used depends on whether its antecedent is a person or a thing.

> **PERSON → *who* or *that***
> Camille is the student *who came for a foreign exchange*.
> Camille → antecedent 3rd. pers. sing.
> who → subject person
> came → verb 3rd pers. sing.
>
> **THING → *which* or *that***
> These are the films *that are most popular*.
> films → antecedent 3rd. pers. pl.
> that → subject thing
> are → verb 3rd. pers. pl.

Combining Sentences with a Relative Pronoun Subject
> **SENTENCE A** The employees were promoted.
> **SENTENCE B** They worked hard.
>
>> 1. Identify the common elements in sentences A and B.
>>   *the employees* and *they* = same people
>>
>> 2. The common element in Sentence A is the antecedent.
>>   *employees* = antecedent
>>
>> 3. The common element in Sentence B is replaced by the relative pronoun.
>>   *they* → relative pronoun

4. The relative pronoun has the same function as the common element in Sentence B.
> *they* = subject of *worked* → relative pronoun = subject of *worked*

5. Choose the relative pronoun according to:
   a. Its function (step 4)
   b. Whether its antecedent (step 2) is a person or a thing
   > *they* = subject referring to a person → *who* or *that*

6. Create the relative clause with relative pronoun (step 5) + remaining elements of Sentence B.
   > *who (that)* worked hard

7. Place the relative clause right after its antecedent (step 2).
   > The employees *who (that) worked hard* were promoted.
   > employees → antecedent

In French

There is only one relative pronoun used as subject of a relative clause → **qui** and the verb agrees with the antecedent of the relative pronoun.

> *This is the teacher who taught me French.*
> Voici l'enseignant qui m'a enseigné le français.
> > l'enseignant → antecedent 3rd pers. sing.
> > qui → subject person
> > a enseigné → verb 3rd. pers. sing.

> *Those are the boxes that are beautiful.*
> Voilà les boîtes qui sont belles.
> > boîtes → antecedent 3rd. pers. pl.
> > qui → subject thing
> > sont → verb 3rd. pers. pl.

Combining Sentences with a Relative Pronoun Subject

Follow the steps above under *In English* (skip 5b).

SENTENCE A	Les employés ont été promus.
	The employees were promoted.
SENTENCE B	Ils ont travaillé dur.
	They worked hard.

Les employés <u>qui ont travaillé dur</u> ont été promus.
The employees <u>who worked hard</u> were promoted.

II. Relative Pronoun as Direct Object
(See *Objects*)

In English
Relative pronouns functioning as direct objects are usually left out in spoken English (the ones in parentheses below). The relative pronoun used will depend on whether the antecedent is a person or a thing.

> **PERSON** → *(whom, who, or that)*
> She is the woman <u>*(whom, who, that)* I met yesterday</u>.
> woman → antecedent
> who → direct object of *met*

> **THING** → *(that, which)*
> That is the book <u>*(that, which)* Maxime recommended</u>.
> book → antecedent
> that, which → direct object of *recommended*

Combining Sentences with a Relative Pronoun Direct Object
Follow the steps above under *In English*.

> **SENTENCE A** The history professor is charismatic.
> **SENTENCE B** I saw him last night.

> 1. Common elements: *history professor* and *him*
> 2. Common element of sentence A: *history professor* → antecedent
> 3. Common element of sentence B: *him* → relative pronoun
> 4. Function of him/relative pronoun: direct object of *saw*
> 5. Relative pronoun: direct object person → *whom, who,* or *that*
> 6. Relative clause: *(whom, who, that)* + *I saw last night*
> 7. Placement of relative clause: after *history teacher*

The history teacher <u>*(whom, who, that)* I saw last night</u> is charismatic.
When the relative pronoun is omitted in spoken English, it is difficult to identify the two clauses (*The history teacher I saw last night is charismatic.*)

In French
Unlike in English, relative pronouns functioning as direct objects are never left out. There is only one relative pronoun used as the direct object of a relative clause → **que** (**qu'** before a vowel).

> *That is the woman **(whom, who, that)** I met yesterday.*
> C'est la femme **que** j'ai rencontré hier.
> > femme → antecedent
> > que → direct object of *rencontré*
>
> *This is the film **(that, which)** he recommends.*
> Voici le film **qu'**il recommande.
> > film → antecedent
> > qu' → direct object of *recommande*

Make sure to check the type of object required by the French verb (see *Relationship of a Verb to Its Object* within the *Objects* chapter).

Agreement of Past Participle: Past participles conjugated with the auxiliary verb **avoir** agree with the direct object if the direct object comes before the verb (see section *Agreement of the Past Participle* in *The Past Tense*). In relative clauses, the direct object pronoun **que** takes on the gender and number of its antecedent, so the past participle must also agree with it in gender and number.

> *Those are the clothes **(that, which)** I purchased.*
> Ce sont les habits **que** j'ai achetés.
> > habits → antecedent masc. pl.
> > achetés → past particle masc. pl. (acheté + s)

Combining Sentences with a Relative Pronoun Direct Object
Follow the steps above under *In English* (skip 5b).

SENTENCE A	Les employés travaillent dur.
	The employees work hard.
SENTENCE B	J'ai rencontré les employés hier.
	I met the employees yesterday.

> *The employees **(that)** I met yesterday work hard.*
> Les employés **que** j'ai rencontrés hier travaillent dur.
> > employés → antecedent masc. pl.
> > rencontrés → past participle masc. pl.

III. Relative Pronoun as an Indirect Object and Object of a Preposition
(see *Objects*)

In English
Relative pronouns functioning as indirect objects or objects of a preposition (shown in parentheses below) are usually left out in spoken English. However, they are used in formal and written English right after the preposition. The relative pronoun used will depend on whether it refers to a person or a thing.

> **PERSON** → **(whom, who, that)** or preposition + **whom**
> She is the teacher *(whom, who, that) I gave my assignment to*. →
> She is the teacher <u>to whom I gave my assignment</u>.
>> teacher → antecedent
>> to whom → indirect object of *gave*
>
> Gérard is the friend *(who, that) I play tennis with*. →
> Gérard is the friend <u>with whom I play tennis</u>.
>> friend → antecedent
>> whom → object of preposition *with*
>
> **THING** → **(that, which)** or preposition + **which**
> We admire the animal shelter *(that, which) we donated to*.
> We admire the animal shelter <u>to which we donated</u>.
>> animal shelter → antecedent
>> which → indirect object of *donated*

Restructuring Sentences with Dangling Prepositions
(See *Dangling Preposition* within the *Interrogative Pronouns* chapter)

To restructure spoken English to formal English, follow these steps:

1. Identify the antecedent.
2. Insert a relative pronoun after the antecedent.
3. Move the dangling preposition from the end of the clause and place it after the antecedent before the relative pronoun.

> Here is the teacher <u>I gave my assignment to</u>. →
> Here is the teacher *(who, that)* I gave my assignment to. →
> Here is the teacher <u>to whom</u> I gave my assignment.
>> teacher → antecedent
>> whom → indirect object of *gave*

The film <u>I was talking *about*</u> is a thriller. →
The film *(that, which)* I was talking about is a thriller. →
The film *about which* I was talking is a thriller.
    film → antecedent
    which → object of preposition *about*

Combining Sentences with a Relative Pronoun as an Indirect Object or as an Object of a Preposition

Follow the steps above under *In English*. Under step 6, move the preposition and place it before the relative pronoun.

SENTENCE A	The employee has arrived.
SENTENCE B	I was waiting for him.

1. Common elements: *employee* and *him*
2. Common element of sentence A: *employee* → antecedent
3. Common element of sentence B: *him* → relative pronoun
4. Function of him/relative pronoun: object of preposition *for*
5. Relative pronoun: object of a preposition → *whom*
6. Create relative clause (preposition + relative pronoun + remainder of sentence B): *for whom I was waiting*
7. Placement of relative clause: *after employee*

Here is the employee <u>*for whom* I was waiting</u>.

SENTENCE A	The book is amazing.
SENTENCE B	I lent it to her.

1. Common elements: *book* and *it*
2. Common element of sentence A: *the book* → antecedent
3. Common element of sentence B: *it* → relative pronoun
4. Function of it/relative pronoun: indirect object of *lent*
5. Relative pronoun: indirect object thing → *which*
6. Create relative clause (preposition + relative pronoun + remainder of sentence B): *which I lent*
7. Placement relative clause: *after book*

The book <u>*which* I lent her</u> is amazing.

In French

Unlike in English, relative pronouns functioning as indirect objects or objects of

181

a preposition are never left out. They follow the rules of formal English. These pronouns are split into two groups based on the preposition required by the French verb or expression:
1. Relative pronouns as objects of a preposition other than the preposition **de**.
2. Relative pronouns as object of the preposition **de**.

Make sure to check the type of object required by the French verb (see *Relationship of a Verb to Its Object* within the *Objects* chapter).

1. French Relative Pronouns as Objects of a Preposition Other Than "DE"
This group includes French verbs that use the preposition **à** *(to)* for indirect objects, and all other prepositions except **de** *(of, about,* etc.). Like in formal English, the relative clause always starts with the preposition followed by a relative pronoun. The relative pronoun used will depend on whether the antecedent is a person or a thing.

PERSON → preposition + qui
Here is the woman (who, that) I was speaking to. →
*Here is the woman **to whom** I was speaking.*
Voici la femme **à qui** je parlais.

THING → preposition + lequel which agrees with the antecedent in gender and number
These are the things (that, which) I work with. →
*These are the things **with which** I work.*
Voici les choses **avec lesquelles** je travaille.
  choses → fem. pl.
  lesquelles → fem. pl.

In addition, following the preposition **à** *(to)* the initial **le-** and **les-** become **au-** and **aux-**.
These are the letters (that, which) we are answering. →
*These are the letters **to which** we are answering.*
Voici les lettres **auxquelles** nous répondons.
  lettres → fem. pl.
  auxquelles → à + fem. pl. (lesquelles)

Combining Sentences with a Relative Pronoun as Indirect Object or Object of a Preposition Other Than "DE"
Follow the steps above under *In English*. Under step 6, use the preposition required by the French verb at the beginning of the relative clause.

SENTENCE A	Elle connaît l'homme.
	She knows the man.
SENTENCE B	Je parle à l'homme.
	I am speaking to the man.

Elle connaît l'homme <u>**à qui** je parle</u>.
*She knows the man **to whom** <u>I speak</u>.*

SENTENCE A	Le lit est grand.
	The bed is large.
SENTENCE B	Ils dorment sur le lit.
	They sleep on the bed.

Le lit <u>**sur lequel** ils dorment</u> est grand.
    lit → masc. sing.
    lequel → masc. sing.

*The bed <u>**on which** they sleep</u> is large.*
    which → object of preposition *on*

2. French Relative Pronouns as Objects of the Preposition "DE"

This group includes French verbs or expressions followed by the preposition **de**. The relative pronoun **dont** replaces the preposition **de** and its object which can refer to either a person or a thing. **Dont** is placed at the beginning of the relative clause.

*The trip <u>**(that, which)** I am dreaming about</u> is expensive.* →
*The trip <u>**about which** I am dreaming</u> is expensive.*
    which → replaces *trip*
    to dream about → rêver de
Le voyage <u>**dont** je rêve</u> est cher.
    dont → replaces *voyage*

Combining Sentences with a Relative Pronoun Object of the Preposition "DE"
Follow the steps above under *In English* (skip 5b).

SENTENCE A	Voici le client.
	Here is the client.
SENTENCE B	Je ne me souviens pas de lui.
	I don't remember him.

Here is the client **(whom, who, that)** I don't remember.
  to remember → se souvenir de

Voici le client **dont** je ne me souviens pas.
  dont → replaces *de lui*

IV. Possessive Relative Pronoun "Whose"

In English
The English relative pronoun *whose* indicates that the antecedent is the possessor of the noun that follows. It can refer to a person or a thing.

  The girl *whose* parents I met.
    the girl's parents → the parents of the girl → whose parents

  I know the building *whose* roof collapsed.
    the building's roof → the roof of the building → whose roof

In French
The equivalent of *whose* is **dont** which can refer to a person or a thing.

SENTENCE A	*This is the girl.*
	Voici la fille.
SENTENCE B	*I met her parents → I met the parents of the girl.*
	J'ai rencontré ses parents. → J'ai rencontré les parents de la fille.

This is the girl **whose** *parents I met.*
Voici la fille **dont** j'ai rencontré les parents.

SENTENCE A	*Look at the building.*
	Regarde le bâtiment.

SENTENCE B	*The roof of the building collapsed.*
	Le toit du bâtiment s'est effondré.

*Look at the building **whose roof collapsed**.*
Regarde le bâtiment **dont** le toit s'est effondré.

Summary of Relative Pronouns with an Antecedent

Here is a chart you can use as reference:

FUNCTION IN RELATIVE CLAUSE	ANTECEDENT	
	PERSON	**THING**
SUBJECT	*who, that*	*which, that*
	qui	qui
DIRECT OBJECT	*whom, who, that*	*that, which*
	que	que
INDIRECT OBJECT & OBJECT OF PREPOSITION OTHER THAN "DE"	*preposition + whom*	*preposition + which*
	prép + qui	prép + lequel
OBJECT OF PREPOSITION "DE"	*preposition + whom*	*preposition + which*
	dont	dont
POSSESSIVE	*whose*	*whose*
	dont	dont

To find the appropriate French relative pronoun, go through the following steps:

1. Restructure the English clause if there is a dangling preposition. Add the relative pronoun, if it has been left out.

2. To choose the correct French relative pronoun, establish the function of the relative pronoun in the French relative clause.
   - If the relative pronoun is the subject → **qui**.
   - If the French verb takes a direct object → **que** or **qu'**. If the French verb is conjugated with **avoir**, make sure the past participle agrees with the

antecedent.
- If the French verb is followed by a preposition other than **de**:
    - If a person → preposition + **qui**
    - If a thing → preposition + appropriate form of **lequel**
- If the French verb or expression is followed by the preposition **de** → **dont**.

3. Placement after the antecedent:
    - If the relative pronoun is the subject or the direct object → relative pronoun + clause.
    - If the relative pronoun is the object of a preposition other than **de** → the preposition + relative pronoun + clause.
    - If the relative pronoun is the object of the preposition de → **dont** + clause.

Let's apply the steps above to the following examples:

*The train **(that, which)** arrives from London is on time.*
1. Relative clause: *that arrives from London*
2. Function of the relative pronoun: subject → **qui**
3. Antecedent: *train* (**train**)
4. Placement: antecedent (**train**) + qui + clause

Le train **qui** arrive de Londres est à temps.

*Here are the groceries **(that, which)** I purchased earlier.*
1. Relative clause: *that I purchased earlier*
2. Function of the relative pronoun: direct object of **acheter** *(to purchase)* → **que**
3. Antecedent: groceries (**courses** = fem. pl.)
4. Placement: antecedent (**courses**) + **que** + clause
5. Agreement of past participle: achetées (fem. pl.)

Voici les courses **que** j'ai achetées tout à l'heure.

*That is the friend **(whom, who, that)** he is staying with.* →
*That is the friend **with whom** he is staying.*
1. Relative clause: *with whom he is staying*
2. Function of the relative pronoun: object of the preposition **avec** *(with)* + person (friend) → **avec qui**
3. Antecedent: *friend* (**ami**)
4. Placement: antecedent (**ami**) + **avec qui** + clause

Voici l'ami **avec qui** il reste.

*Where is the assignment **(that, which)** she's working on?* →
*Where is the assignment **on which** she's working?*
1. Relative clause: *on which she's working*

2. Function of the relative pronoun: object of preposition **sur** *(on)* + thing *(assignment)*
3. Antecedent: *assignment* (**devoir** = masculine singular)
4. Placement: antecedent (**devoir**) + **sur lequel** + clause

Où est le devoir **sur lequel** elle travaille ?

Where are the tools (that, which) you need?
1. Relative clause: *that you need*
2. Function of the relative pronoun: object of preposition **de** *(to need → avoir besoin de)*
3. Selection: **dont**
4. Antecedent: *tools* (**outils**)
5. Placement: antecedent (**outils**) + **dont** + clause

Où sont les outils **dont** tu as besoin ?

Relative Pronouns without an Antecedent

There are relative pronouns that do not refer to a specific noun or pronoun. Instead, they refer to an antecedent that has not been expressed or to an entire idea.

In English
Some relative pronouns can be used without an antecedent: ***what, which, that.***

- To refer to an unspecified thing or event → ***what***
    I don't know *what* is going to happen.
        what → no antecedent object

    Here is *what* I know.
        what → no antecedent direct object

- To refer to an entire idea expressed in a preceding clause → comma + ***which*** or ***that***
    He isn't feeling well, *which* is unfortunate.
        which → antecedent: the fact that he isn't feeling well subject of *is*

    To gain muscle fast, *that* is what I strive for.
        that → antecedent: the fact that the person wants to gain muscle fast subject of *is*

Careful – Don't confuse the relative pronoun *what* with other uses of *what*: as an interrogative pronoun (*What are you looking for?* Qu'est-ce que tu cherches ?), and as an interrogative adjective (*What cake do you want?* Quel gâteau voulez-vous ?).

In French

When a relative pronoun does not have a specific antecedent or refers to an idea, the pronoun **ce** *(that)* is added to act as the antecedent. It is followed by the correct relative pronoun for its function in the relative clause.

Here are a few examples.

> *Here is **what is going to happen**.*
> 1. Relative clause: *what is going to happen*
> 2. No antecedent: add **ce**
> 3. Function: subject of **va arriver** *(going to happen)* → **ce qui**
>
> Voici **ce qui** va arriver.

> *She doesn't speak English, **which may be problematic**.*
> 1. Relative clause: *which may be problematic*
> 2. Antecedent: she doesn't speak English → add **ce**
> 3. Function: subject of **pourrait être** *(may be)* → **ce qui**
>
> Elle ne parle pas anglais, **ce qui** pourrait être problématique.

> *Tell me **what she did**.*
> 1. Relative clause: *what she did*
> 2. No antecedent: add **ce**
> 3. Function: direct object of **a fait** *(did)* → **ce que**
>
> Dites-moi **ce qu'**elle a fait.

> *I don't understand **what you're dreaming about**.*
> 1. Relative clause: *what you're dreaming about* → Restructured: *about what you are dreaming*
> 2. No antecedent: add **ce**
> 3. Function: object of preposition **de** *(to dream about* → rêver de*)* → **ce dont**
>
> Je ne comprends pas **ce dont** tu rêves.

FRENCH FACT: VERLAN

Verlan is a French "backslang" mostly spoken and used by French youth. It is a playful linguistic trick where the syllables of a word are reversed. For example, **l'envers** becomes **verlan** *(backslang)*, **femme** *(woman)* becomes **meuf**, and **merci** *(thank you)* becomes **cimer**. Learning verlan can be a fun way to dive into French slang and culture.

Chapter 44: Demonstrative Pronouns

> **ILLUSTRATIVE EXAMPLE**
>
> English: **This** is the book I was talking about, **these** are the pictures from my trip, and **that** is the souvenir I brought back for you.
>
> French: **Ceci** est le livre dont je parlais, **celles-ci** sont les photos de mon voyage, et **cela** est le souvenir que j'ai ramené pour toi.

A **Demonstrative Pronoun** is a word that replaces a noun as if it's pointing to it. The word demonstrative comes from *demonstrate*, to show.

> Choose a <u>dress</u>. *This one* is sexy. *That one* is modest.
>   dress → antecedent
>   this one → points to one dress
>   that one → points to another dress

In English and in French demonstrative pronouns can be used in a variety of ways.

This One, That One and These, Those

In English

The singular forms of the demonstrative pronouns are ***this*** (one) and ***that*** (one); the plural forms are ***these*** and ***those***.

> Here are the <u>plates</u>. *This one* is clean; *those* are dirty.
>   plates → antecedent
>   this one → singular
>   those → plural

> Choose a <u>film</u>. *These* are in English, *that one* is in French.
>   film → antecedent
>   these → plural
>   that one → singular

This (one) / these refer to persons or things near the speaker, and *that (one) / those* refer to persons or things further away from the speaker.

In French

Demonstrative pronouns agree in gender with their **antecedent** (the noun to which they refer). Their number depends on whether they refer to one person or thing (*this one, that one*) or to more than one person or thing (*these, those*). Also, **-ci** is added to indicate persons or things close to the speaker, and **-là** to indicate persons or things further away.

		MASCULINE	FEMININE
SINGULAR	*this, that (one)*	celui-ci, celui-là	celle-ci, celle-là
PLURAL	*these, those (ones)*	ceux-ci, ceux-là	celles-ci, celles-là

To choose the correct form, follow these steps:
1. Find the antecedent.
2. Determine the gender of the antecedent.
3. Number: *this one, that one* → singular; *these, those* → plural.
4. Based on steps 2 and 3, choose the correct form from the chart above.
5. Add **-ci** for *this* or *these* and **-là** for *that* and *those*.

Look at the following examples:

Which film did you watch? ***This one.***
Quel film as-tu vu ? **Celui-ci.**
1. Antecedent: film
2. Gender: **film** (*film*) → masculine
3. Number: this one → singular
4. Selection: **celui**
5. This → **-ci**

Which brochure did you take? ***That one.***
Quelle brochure as-tu prise? **Celle-là.**
1. Antecedent: brochure
2. Gender: **brochure** (*brochure*) → feminine
3. Number: that one → singular
4. Selection: **celle**
5. That → **-là**

Which shops did you go to? ***These.***
À quels magasins as-tu été ? **Ceux-ci.**
1. Antecedent: shops
2. Gender: **magasins** (*shops*) → masculine
3. Number: these → plural
4. Selection: **ceux**
5. These → **-ci**

Which flowers did you buy? ***Those.***
Quelles fleurs as-tu achetées ? **Celles-là.**
1. Antecedent: flowers
2. Gender: **fleurs** *(flowers)* → feminine
3. Number: those → plural
4. Selection: **celles**
5. Those → **-là**

To Show Possession: "Celui de"
(see also *The Possessive*)

In English
You can show possession with an apostrophe after the possessor, without repeating the person or thing possessed that is mentioned in a previous sentence. The person or thing possessed is the antecedent.

> Do you have a bicycle? No, I use my *girlfriend's*.
> bicycle → antecedent
> girlfriend's → possessor + apostrophe
> The word *bicycle* is not repeated after *girlfriend*, it is implied.

In French
Remember that the apostrophe structure to show possession does not exist in French. For the same reason that *my girlfriend's bicycle* can only be expressed through the structure *the bicycle of my girlfriend*, the expression *my girlfriend's* can only be expressed through a structure without an apostrophe. This structure word-for-word corresponds to *the one of* (singular antecedent) or *the ones of* (plural antecedent).

> Do you have a <u>bicycle</u>? No, I use my *girlfriend's*.
> bicycle → singular
> girlfriend's → possessor + apostrophe *(the one of my girlfriend)*

> Did you bring your <u>keys</u>? No, but I brought my *mother's*.
> keys → plural
> mother's → possessor + apostrophe *(the ones of my mother)*

To show possession when the person or thing possessed is not stated in the same sentence, French uses the demonstrative pronouns (without **-ci** or **-là**) + **de** *(of)*.

To choose the correct form, follow these steps:

1. Find the antecedent of *the one* or *the ones*.
2. Determine the gender and number of the antecedent.
3. Based on step 2, select the form of the demonstrative pronoun on the chart above.
4. Add the preposition **de** *(of)*.

Let's apply these rules to the following examples:

*Which <u>car</u> are you fixing? **My uncle's.***
Quelle <u>voiture</u> réparez-vous ? **Celle de mon oncle.**
　　1. Antecedent: car (voiture)
　　2. Gender & number: **voiture** *(car)* → feminine singular
　　3. Demonstrative pronoun: **celle**
　　4. Selection: **celle de**

*Which <u>books</u> are you throwing away? **The old lady's.***
Quels <u>livres</u> jetez-vous ? **Ceux de la vieille dame.**
　　1. Antecedent: books (livres)
　　2. Gender & number: **livres** *(books)* → masculine plural
　　3. Demonstrative pronoun: **ceux**
　　4. Selection: **ceux de**

The One (That): Celui qui, Celui que
(see *Relative Pronouns*)

In English
The pronouns *the one* (for singular) and *the ones* (for plural), followed by the relative pronouns *that, which,* or *who*, can start a relative clause that provides more information about a person or thing mentioned in a previous sentence. Since *that, which,* or *who* are often left out in English, we have put them in parentheses.

What car are you purchasing? *The one (that) you recommended me.*
　　Clause: *the one that you recommended me*
　　　　additional information about the car
　　Number: *The one* is singular.

Which family members went to France? *The ones (who) are learning French.*
　　Clause: *the ones who are learning French*
　　　　additional information about the family members
　　Number: *The ones* is plural.

In French

To express the English structure above, French uses the demonstrative pronouns followed by a relative pronoun.
- The demonstrative pronouns agree in gender and number with the antecedent.
- The relative pronoun is selected according to its function in the relative clause.

To choose the correct form, follow these steps:

A. Demonstrative pronoun *(the one, the ones)*
1. Find the antecedent.
2. Determine the gender and number of the antecedent.
3. Select the French form.

B. Relative pronoun *(that, which, who → add to the English sentence if it has been omitted)*
1. Determine the function of the relative pronoun in the relative clause.
2. Select the correct French form based on step 1:
   - Subject → **qui**
   - Object → **que**

Let's apply these rules to the following examples:

What films are you watching? **The ones (that)** *you recommended me.*
A. Demonstrative pronoun *(the ones)*
1. Antecedent: films (films)
2. Gender & number: **films** *(films)* → masculine plural
3. Selection: **ceux**

B. Relative pronoun *(that)*
1. Function: *that* is the object of the relative clause.
2. (Answers the question: *"You recommended what?"* You is the subject.)
3. Selection: **que**

Quels films regardes-tu ? **Ceux que** tu m'as recommandés.
1. films → antecedent, masc. pl.
2. ceux que → demonstrative pronoun masc. pl. + relative pronoun object
3. Note: The past participle **recommandés** agrees with the direct object **films** (masc. pl.) which precedes it (see *Agreement of the Past Participle* in The Past Tense chapter).

Which women went to France? **The ones who** *are learning French.*
A. Demonstrative pronoun *(the ones)*
1. Antecedent: women (femmes)

      2.   Gender & number: **femmes** *(women)* → feminine plural
      3.   Selection: **celles**

B. Relative pronoun *(who)*
    1.   Function: *who* is the subject of the relative clause.
    2.   Selection: **qui**

Quelles sont les <u>femmes</u> qui sont parties en France ? **<u>Celles qui</u>** apprennent le français.
        femmes → antecedent fem. pl.
        celles qui → demonstrative pronoun fem. pl. + relative pronoun subject

---

FRENCH FACT: PUNCTUATION

French punctuation rules differ from English. For instance, in French, a space is placed before punctuation marks like colons, semicolons, exclamation marks, and question marks. For example: **Bonjour ! Comment ça va ?** *(Good morning! How are you?)*

Chapter 45: Active and Passive Voice

> **ILLUSTRATIVE EXAMPLE**
>
> English: *She **wrote** the letter in the morning, and it **was delivered** by the postman the next day, ensuring her message **reached** its destination on time.*
>
> French: *Elle **a écrit** la lettre le matin, et elle **a été livrée** par le facteur le lendemain, assurant que son message **atteigne** sa destination à temps.*

Voice in the grammatical sense refers to the relationship between the verb and its subject. There are two voices, the **Active Voice** and the **Passive Voice.**

Active Voice – A sentence is said to be in the active voice when the subject is the performer of the action of the verb. In this instance, the verb is called an **Active Verb.**

> The professor *corrects* the exams.
>   professor → subject
>   corrects → verb
>   the exams → direct object
>
> Myriam *ate* an apricot.
>   Myriam → subject
>   ate → verb
>   apricot → direct object
>
> Rain *has flooded* the street.
>   rain → subject
>   has flooded → verb
>   the street → direct object
>
> The police officer *gave* a fine to the gentleman.
>   police officer → subject
>   gave → verb
>   fine → direct object
>   to the gentleman → indirect object

In all the examples above, the subject performs the action of the verb and the direct object or the indirect object is the receiver of the action (see *Subjects* and *Objects*).

Passive Voice – A sentence is said to be in the passive voice when the subject is the receiver of the action of the verb. In this instance, the verb is called a **Passive Verb.**

The exams *are corrected* by the professor.
    exams → subject
    are corrected → verb
    professor → agent

The apricot *was eaten* by Myriam.
    apricot → subject
    was eaten → verb
    Myriam → agent

The street *has been flooded* by the rain.
    street → subject
    has been flooded → verb
    rain → agent

The gentleman *was given* a fine by the police officer.
    gentleman → subject
    was given → verb
    fine → direct object
    police officer → agent

In all the examples above, the subject is the receiver of the action of the verb. The performer of the action (if mentioned) is introduced by the word *by* and is called the **Agent**.

In English

The passive voice is expressed by the auxiliary verb *to be* conjugated in the different tenses + the past participle of the main verb (see *Participles*). The tense of the passive sentence is determined by the tense of the verb *to be*.

    The exams ***are** corrected* by the professor.
        are → present

    The exams ***were** corrected* by the professor.
        were → past

    The exams ***will be** corrected* by the professor.
        will be → future

A direct or an indirect object of the verb can function as the subject of the passive sentence.

    The *exams* were corrected by the professor.
        exams → subject

the professor corrected the exams → direct object in the active sentence

The *exams* were corrected for the students by the professor.
exams → subject
The professor corrected the exams for *the students* → indirect object in the active sentence

While the use of the passive voice is very common in English, it is mostly avoided in French.

In French
Same as in English, a passive verb is expressed with the auxiliary **être** *(to be)* conjugated in the appropriate tense + the past participle of the main verb. The tense of the passive sentence is determined by the tense of the verb **être**.

Les examens **sont** corrigés par le professeur.
sont → present
*The exams **are** corrected by the professor.*

Les examens **ont été** corrigés par le professeur.
ont été → past
*The exams **(have been) were** corrected by the professor.*

Les examens **seront** corrigés par le professeur.
seront → future
*The exams **will be** corrected by the professor.*

Since the past participles of passive verbs are always conjugated with the auxiliary verb **être**, they always agree in gender and number with the subject (see *Agreement of the Past Participle* in *The Past Tense* chapter).

Les **pâtisseries** françaises sont **connues** à travers le monde.
pâtisseries → subject fem. pl.
connues → past participle fem. pl.
*French **pastries** are **known** throughout the world.*

Unlike in English, in French, only the direct object of a verb can function as the subject in a passive sentence. If the verb has an indirect object, French avoids the passive voice and uses the **on** construction instead.

Avoiding the Passive Voice in French

If the agent is mentioned, the passive sentence is turned into an active sentence.

1. The agent of the passive sentence introduced with *by* becomes the subject of the active sentence, and the subject of the passive sentence is made the direct object of the active sentence.

PASSIVE	*The exams are corrected **by the professor**.*
	[S] [agent]
	Les examens sont corrigés par **le professeur**.
ACTIVE	*The professor corrects the exams.*
	[S] [DO]
	Le professeur corrige **les examens**.

2. The tense of the verb *to be* in the passive sentence is reflected in the active sentence.

PASSIVE (PRESENT)	*The exams **are corrected** by the professor.*
	Les examens **sont corrigés** par le professeur.
ACTIVE (PRÉSENT)	*The professor **corrects** the exams.*
	Le professeur **corrige** les examens.

PASSIVE (PAST)	*The exams **were corrected** by the professor.*
	Les examens **ont été corrigés** par le professeur.
ACTIVE (PASSÉ COMPOSÉ)	*The professor **corrected** the exams.*
	Le professeur **a corrigé** les examens.

PASSIVE (FUTURE)	*The exams **will be corrected** by the professor.*
	Les examens **seront corrigés** par le professeur.
ACTIVE (FUTUR)	*The professor **will correct** the exams.*
	Le professeur **corrigera** les examens.

If the agent is not mentioned in the passive sentence, there are two possible constructions to avoid the passive.

1. **Reflexive Verb Construction** – The main verb of the sentence is changed to a reflexive verb (see *Reflexive Pronouns and Verbs*). This reflexive construction

is used primarily for general statements.

*The meals **are prepared** in advance.*
Les repas **se préparent** à l'avance.

*The Camel cigarettes **are bought** here.*
Les cigarettes Camel **s'achètent** ici.

2. "On" Construction – The pronoun **on** is added to serve as the subject of an active sentence. In this instance, **on** corresponds to the English indefinite pronoun *one*, as in the sentence, *One should eat when one is hungry.*

*A basic level of math **is taught** in all schools.*
> Math, the subject, is not doing the teaching: therefore, the sentence is in the passive voice.

On enseigne un niveau basique de mathématiques dans toutes les écoles.
> On, the subject, is doing the teaching; therefore, the sentence is in the active voice.

*Lasagna **was cooked** for dinner.*
> Lasagna, the subject, was not doing the cooking; therefore, the sentence is in the passive voice.

On a cuisiné de la lasagne pour le dîner.
> On, the subject, was doing the cooking: therefore, the sentence is in the active voice.

In addition, the pronoun **on** is added to serve as the subject of an active sentence in order to avoid a passive sentence with an indirect object as subject.

PASSIVE	*The family was given money.* The family → subject (money was given to the family → IO in active sentence)
ACTIVE	**On** a donné de l'argent à la famille. On → subject (word-for-word: *one gave money to the family*)

Careful – Remember that in the active voice, verbs form their past tenses with either **être** *(to be)* or **avoir** *(to have)* as auxiliary (see *The Past Tense*). French verbs that form their past tenses with the auxiliary **être** in the active voice cannot be made passive.

> **FRENCH FACT: ACCENTS**
>
> French uses several unique accents, such as the acute accent (é), grave accent (è, à), circumflex (ê, â, ô, û), diaeresis (ë), and cedilla (ç), each altering pronunciation and meaning.

Download the Audiobook & PDF below and get access to our online French Course!

www.ingramcontent.com/pod-product-compliance
Lightning Source LLC
Chambersburg PA
CBHW072051110526
44590CB00018B/3122